W9-BZC-193

Culture and Customs of Russia

Culture and Customs of Russia

∾⚬∾

Sydney Schultze

Conard High School Library
West Hartford, Conn.

GREENWOOD PRESS
Westport, Connecticut • London

105417

947
SCH

Library of Congress Cataloging-in-Publication Data

Schultze, Sydney.
     Culture and customs of Russia / Sydney Schultze.
        p.   cm.
     Includes bibliographical references and index.
     ISBN 0–313–31101–3 (alk. paper)
     1. Russia (Federation)—Civilization.   2. Russia (Federation)—Social life and customs.   I. Title.
   DK510.32.S37   2000
   947—dc21   00–034135

British Library Cataloguing in Publication Data is available.

Copyright © 2000 by Sydney Schultze

All rights reserved. No portion of this book may be
reproduced, by any process or technique, without
the express written consent of the publisher.

Library of Congress Catalog Card Number: 00–034135
ISBN: 0–313–31101–3 $46.95

First published in 2000

Greenwood Press, 88 Post Road West, Westport, CT 06881
An imprint of Greenwood Publishing Group, Inc.
www.greenwood.com

Printed in the United States of America

∞

The paper used in this book complies with the
Permanent Paper Standard issued by the National
Information Standards Organization (Z39.48–1984).

10 9 8 7 6 5 4 3 2

All photographs appear by courtesy of the author, Sydney Schultze.

For Adrian, Jack, Tom

Contents

CONTENTS

A photo essay follows p. 76

Acknowledgments

I WOULD LIKE to thank Tom Buser, my husband, for his generous help and encouragement at every single stage of this project. I would also like to thank Bruce Adams and Christine Rydel for reading the manuscript, Nancy Alexander for assistance in converting slides to photo images, my editors Wendi Schnaufer and Rebecca Ardwin for their support, and the University of Louisville College of Arts and Sciences for its research grant.

A Note on Spelling

THIS BOOK uses common popular spellings rather than adhering to a single style of transliteration. The reader should note that Russian words can be rendered in English in various ways. The name Tolstoy, for instance, may also be spelled Tolstoi or Tolstoj. Dostoevsky might be spelled Dostoevskii, Dostoyevsky, or Dostoevskij.

Chronology of the History of Russia

Prehistoric Period	Evidence of habitation in Stone Age
1200 B.C.–A.D. 800	Successive invasions north of Black Sea by Cimmerians, Scythians, Sarmatians, Goths, Huns, Avars; Khazars near Volga; Slavs move into the area now called Russia
863	Cyril and Methodius create an alphabet; successor to this alphabet will be called Cyrillic
800s	Rise of Kiev, formation of Russian state
988	Vladimir Christianizes Russia
1147	First mention of Moscow in the chronicles
1240	Kiev falls to Mongols
1380	Battle of Kulikovo
1480	Ivan III, the Great, ends Mongol rule
1547	Ivan IV, the Terrible, is the first to have himself crowned tsar of Russia
1604–1613	Time of Troubles
1613	Romanov dynasty begins
1682–1725	Peter I, the Great, rules

1703	Peter I founds St. Petersburg, which will replace Moscow as the capital until the Communist era
1762–1796	Catherine II, the Great, rules
1770s	Peasant revolt
1799	Birth of Alexander Pushkin, father of Russian literature
1812	Napoleon invades Russia
1825	Decembrist revolt
1825–1855	Nicholas I rules
1861	Serfs are emancipated during the rule of Alexander II
1881	Alexander II assassinated
1905	Japan defeats Russia in Russo-Japanese War; general strike; Duma (parliament) founded
1914	World War I begins
1917	Russian revolution; communists seize power later that year; Vladimir Lenin begins rule
1918	Tsar Nicholas II and his family murdered
1924	Lenin dies; Stalin will gain power and rule until 1953
1930s	Stalin's purges
1941	Germany invades Russia; World War II ends 1945
1957	Russia launches Sputnik, beginning the space age; Yuri Gagarin will orbit earth in 1961; Russia will launch space station Mir in 1986
1958–1964	Nikita Khrushchev rules
1964–1982	Leonid Brezhnev rules; this will be known as the era of stagnation
1985–1991	Rule of Mikhail Gorbachev, who attempts to bring *perestroika* (rebuilding) and *glasnost* (openness) to Russia

1991   Communism ends in Russia

1991–1999   Boris Yeltsin heads the government; Russia suffers as it tries to move to a capitalist system; Yeltsin attempts to crush independence movement in Chechnya; he resigns voluntarily at the end of 1999

2000   Vladimir Putin, Yeltsin's prime minister, takes over

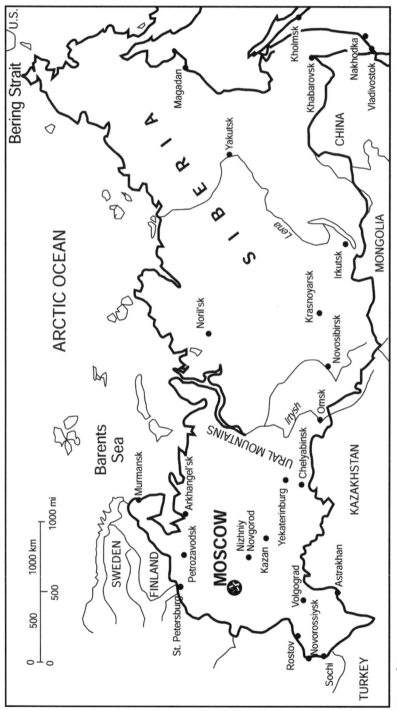

Map of Russia.

1

The Land, People, and History

THE LAND

IN 1991, the Union of Soviet Socialist Republics disintegrated. The Russian empire that stretched from Poland to the Pacific suddenly lost much of the land acquired over centuries of expansion. No longer could one look at a map of "Russia" and include the Baltic Sea republics of Estonia, Latvia, and Lithuania; in the south, Armenia, Georgia, and Azerbaijan; in the west, Moldova; or the five "stans" in central Asia, Uzbekistan, Tajikistan, Kyrgyzstan, Kazakhstan, and Turkmenistan. Even the other East Slavic–speaking lands of Belarus (which means "white Russia") and Ukraine (which means "borderland," also known as "little Russia") could no longer be thought of as part of the Russian empire. Russia nominally still belonged to, and to some extent dominated, a postcommunist entity called the Commonwealth of Independent States, but that was a very fluid and loosely organized arrangement and could not really be thought of as a unified country any longer.

Russia (*Rossiia*), or Russian Federation (*Rossiiskaia Federatsiia*) as it is officially called, seems almost shrunken on the new maps, yet it is still the largest country in the world, with a total of 6,592,741 square miles, nearly 1.8 times the size of the United States. Distances are huge. Americans travel from Maine to California and cross four time zones. Russia spreads across eleven time zones, sprawling nearly halfway around the world. Population centers are linked by air, rail, water, and road, although the roads are often poor. Riding the Trans-Siberian railway is one of the great rail adventures in the world, crossing thousands of miles on a six-day journey across most of

Russia from Moscow to Vladivostok (which means "power of the east"), passing through the major cities of Perm, Ekaterinburg, Omsk, Novosibirsk, and Irkutsk.

The country spans two continents, Europe and Asia, and shares borders with several of the former republics as well as with Norway, Finland, Poland, China, Mongolia, and Korea. Much of Russia is rather flat, with some mountainous areas in the eastern part, which is called Siberia. The two best-known mountain ranges are the Urals, low mountains separating Europe from Asia, and the beautiful Caucasus Mountains, which lie on the southern border between the Black Sea and the Caspian Sea. The tallest mountain in Russia is Mt. Elbrus in the Caucasus, at 18,481 feet. In the east, Kamchatka peninsula, part of the Pacific ring of fire, is home to numerous volcanoes.

Russia lies much farther north than the United States, more on a level with Canada. The far northern part of Russia is quite cold and has little sunlight in the winter. With its permanently frozen subsoil, or permafrost, this area is inhospitable to large plants like trees. The land north of the tree line is known as the tundra. In the south lies the steppe, or open prairie, which provides some good land for agriculture. In between the tundra and the steppe is the taiga, or forest land, the largest coniferous forest in the world. The most common tree is the larch, although there are many other kinds of trees, such as spruce and pine.

Russians have a deep love for nature, particularly for their forest. Russia has even been known as "wooden Russia" because so much of it was built of wood. Their most beloved tree is the birch tree, with its distinctive white black-flecked trunk. Russian movies and books are full of references to the birch tree, and even stores where foreigners shopped were named *beriozka*, or little birch tree in communist times. Some of the economy has depended on logging, but at the same time, Russians have long been aware of the necessity to preserve their forest land. A hundred years ago, playwright Anton Chekhov addressed this problem in his play *Uncle Vanya*.

Rainfall in Russia is greatest in the summer, although annual rainfall ranges only 16–32 inches in the west and even less in the northeast and south central areas. Russians are used to a lot of snow in the winter and have at least three different words for blizzard. They have been known to express disappointment if a winter is unseasonably mild and lacking in snow.

Russia is traversed by several major rivers. In the west flows the Volga, the longest river in Europe. Interconnected waterways, including the Volga, make it possible to go by water from St. Petersburg on the Gulf of Finland to Moscow, then eventually all the way to the Caspian Sea, a salt lake which is the largest inland body of water in the world. Other long rivers in western

Russia include the Don and the Pechora. In Siberia, the Ob-Irtysh, the Lena, and the Yenisei flow north to the Arctic. Russia also has several large lakes. In the west are Lake Ladoga and Lake Onega, the largest lakes in Europe. Siberia's Lake Baikal, the deepest lake in the world, contains more than one-fifth of the world's unfrozen fresh water. Russia long sought to have seaports from which to trade. The northern ports are frozen much of the year, and eastern ports are far from the population centers in European Russia. Russia does have ports on the Baltic and the Black seas, and thus indirect access to the Mediterranean and Atlantic.

Russia's animal population is varied, including the bear, reindeer, elk, and Siberian tiger. Russia is famous for its luxurious furs from animals such as the sable and fox. Its natural resources are extensive and abundant: iron, copper, zinc, mercury, gas, coal, tin, silver, diamonds, and gold, among others.

POPULATION

The population of Russia in mid-1998 was estimated at 146,861,022 and appeared to be slightly decreasing because more deaths than births were being recorded (9.57 births and 14.89 deaths per 1,000 people). Life expectancy for women is about seventy-one years; for men it is an alarming fifty-eight. More male babies are born than female babies and there are more males than females under the age of fifteen, but there are more females than males over the age of fifteen.

Most of the people who live in Russia are ethnic Russians, although nearly one-fifth claim other ethnic backgrounds: 81.5 percent are Russian, 3.8 percent are Tatar, 3 percent are Ukrainian, 1.2 percent are Chuvash, 0.9 percent are Bashkir, 0.8 percent are Belarussian, while other small groups such as the Yakuts, Chechens, Mari, Mordva, Jews, Germans, Udmurt, and others make up the rest of the population. They speak a wide variety of languages. Eighteen million are Muslim, but there are other religions as well, including shamanism. Within the Russian Federation are numerous republics representing various groups or nationalities, although ethnic Russians outnumber the other groups in about half of them. After the fall of communism, some of these groups like the Bashkirs and Tatars negotiated for more rights within the Federation, while the Chechens fought for independence.

Three-fourths of the population live in urban areas. The population is much denser in European Russia than in the area beyond the Urals. The largest city is Moscow, the capital, with a population of 8,793,000. Second largest is St. Petersburg, called Leningrad in communist times, with a population of 4,883,000. About a dozen other cities have populations of over 1,000,000. Moscow is very lively, a busy, colorful city, where nearly everything is available, though it may be costly. St. Petersburg is more elegant, more European, and thinks of itself as more civilized and cultured than Moscow. These cities, the "two capitals" (St. Petersburg was the capital for two centuries before the 1917 revolution), are the cultural centers of the country. Amenities are fewer in the smaller cities, and even more scarce in the villages.

RUSSIAN LANGUAGE

Russian is an Indo-European language, a large group of languages that includes English, German, French, and Spanish, as well as many other languages spoken in a wide area stretching from India to Europe. Because these languages are related, many common everyday words in the languages are similar. For instance, the Russian word *brat* means brother, *sestra* means sister, and *mat* means mother. Russian also shares with English words that both languages borrowed from French and other languages of Western Europe. The Russian words *matematika, literatura,* and *biologiia* are only a few of the many examples of words of this sort. English has borrowed only a few words from Russian, like "vodka" and "tsar," but recently Russian has been borrowing a very large number of words from English, particularly words associated with business, but also words connected with American culture, like *rok* (rock).

Russian belongs to a subgroup of Indo-European languages called Slavic. In the Slavic subgroup are languages such as Polish, Czech, Slovak, and Bulgarian. Russian is close to these languages, but even closer to other East Slavic languages like Ukrainian and Belarussian.

Russian is written in a different alphabet, called Cyrillic. Two Slavs named Cyril and Methodius attempted to create an alphabet for the Slavic people to facilitate the spread of Christianity in the ninth century. This alphabet was superseded by another, easier alphabet which became known as Cyrillic, in honor of Cyril. The Cyrillic alphabet is based on Greek, with the addition of extra letters. Here is what the alphabet looks like: а б в г д е ё ж з и й к л м н о п р с т у ф х ц ч ш щ ъ ы ь э ю я The letters а к м о т are the same as English. Some letters are tricky for English speakers: the Russian в is our "v," г is "g," н is "n," and р is "r." The language is mostly phonetic, meaning that what you see on the page is what you say, unlike English, which has silent letters like the gh in "thought."

In some ways Russian is difficult, but in other ways it is easy. Russian has a very large vocabulary. It also has a very complex system of putting different letters on the end of nouns to show whether the noun is the subject, the direct object, or the possessive, or just what it is doing in the sentence. On the other hand, the verb system is much simpler than English. The verbs are easy to form and do not have as many tenses as English. In addition, Russian has no words for "the" or "a" and no word to express the present tense of "to be." While we might say "This is a book," Russians can get by with two words, *Eto kniga* (This—book.)

Russians are proud of their language, which they rightly consider very expressive and beautiful, in both oral and written form. In this language they have created one of the greatest literatures of the world, particularly in the genre of the novel.

EARLY HISTORY

Russia has a long, turbulent, exciting history. There is evidence that people lived in Russia as long ago as the Stone Age. Much later, about 3,000 years ago, the area north of the Black Sea was inhabited by a group called the Cimmerians. They were conquered by invaders known as the Scythians about 700 B.C. The Scythians, nomads from Central Asia, left behind gold ornaments that show that they were not only fine warriors but had an eye for beauty as well. The Scythians were eventually defeated by the Sarmatians, who were followed in the next several centuries by the Goths, the Huns, and the Avars. Yet another group, the Khazars, eventually took over the area near the mouth of the Volga.

Sometime in the dim past, the Slavs began occupying eastern Europe, including the area that would become part of Russia. No one is really sure where these Slavs originally came from, but they are the ancestors of our modern Russians. By the mid 800s, the Slavs were busily engaged in trade and had built several towns. Kiev was particularly successful and became the first of the three major capitals in Russian history; the others were Moscow and St. Petersburg. Much of what we know about Kiev and the other settlements comes from Kiev's *Tale of Bygone Years*, or *Primary Chronicle*, which is part history and part legend. According to a legend in the *Chronicle*, Kiev was founded by three brothers Kii, Shchek, and Khoriv, who had a sister Lybed. The city was named after the oldest brother.

The *Chronicle* also states that the Slavs fought among themselves and decided to invite the Vikings, or Varangians as the Russians call them, to establish order and rule over them. The town of Novgorod, according to this account, invited the Varangian Rus leader Rurik to be their ruler in 862 and members of his party, Askold and Dir, took over the rule of Kiev. The word *Rus*, the *Chronicle* states, gave rise to the word Russia. Although the Varangians were indeed present in the area, it is not certain that they were "invited" to rule, or that there were real people named Rurik, Askold, and Dir, or even that the name Russia comes from the word Rus. A few historians think that the Varangians just seized power and that the name Russia comes from the name of a southern group of Slavs.

The *Chronicle* states that when Rurik died, he handed over power to his relative Oleg, who moved the seat of government to Kiev in 882. Oleg really did exist and is the first nonlegendary ruler. Oleg and his successor Igor strove to increase the power and authority of Kiev, which lay at a very advantageous location on the Russian waterway system that led from Scandinavia to the Black Sea and Constantinople. Kiev exported such products as furs, wax, and honey down this waterway.

The *Chronicle* tells some wonderful stories about Oleg and Igor. It seems that a soothsayer told Oleg that his horse would cause his death. Oleg stayed away from the horse, but when it died, he scornfully stepped on its skull. A snake came out of the skull and bit him, causing his death. When Igor was killed by his enemies, the Derevlians, his widow Olga pretended to agree to marry their ruler. Instead she tricked them and engaged in very colorful forms of revenge, including tying matches to little birds she had asked for in tribute. When the birds were released, they flew back home, setting fire to all the Derevlians' houses.

Olga converted to Christianity, and her grandson Vladimir chose to adopt Christianity as the official religion in 988, replacing the pagan religion of most of the inhabitants of Kiev. Vladimir chose the Christianity of Constantinople rather than Rome, that is, the eastern branch of the church which would soon become the Orthodox Church, rather than the western branch that would become Catholicism. This was a very significant event, because it tied Kiev culturally to southeastern Europe rather than to western Europe or to Asia. This decision would influence Russia's development in profound ways over the next thousand years.

The next century and a half marked a kind of golden age for Kiev. This was the time of good rulers such as Yaroslav the Wise and Vladimir Monomakh, a time with a few periods of peace and a flowering of culture. Compared with many other European towns, Kiev's cultural level was rather high. Art and literature flourished, with even the rulers producing works of literature. The legal system was noteworthy for favoring punishment by fines rather than capital punishment.

Yet wars, changing trade routes, and internal struggles between the various

Russian towns were weakening Kiev. Other towns, like Novgorod, Pskov, Vladimir, and Suzdal, grew in relative importance. Today, Suzdal is tiny, rising like a fairy city with its onion domes in the midst of a great green meadow. Vladimir and Novgorod are also comparatively small. But in the twelfth century, Suzdal and Vladimir were thriving political and cultural centers northeast of Kiev. In the northwest, Novgorod had achieved independence and was selecting its own leaders, whose powers were very limited. In 1147, another northern town, Moscow, is first mentioned in the chronicles.

THE FALL OF KIEV AND THE RISE OF MOSCOW

With Kiev weakened and central authority in disarray, suddenly a terrible disaster struck, an event so devastating that some Russians think its effects are still felt today. Genghis Khan had established a powerful Mongol Empire far to the east, and after his death in 1227, his descendants continued his efforts to expand control over much of Asia and on into Europe. The Mongols swept down out of Asia in 1237 and destroyed many Russian towns, burning and killing as they went. Kiev fell in 1240, effectively ending the Kievan age in Russian history. The Mongols initially were able to take control of all Russia except the Novgorod region, but even this area was later forced to submit to Mongol authority.

The Mongols formed a state called the Golden Horde; its center was at Sarai, northwest of the Caspian Sea. The Russian rulers, the princes of the various regions, had to travel there to pledge their loyalty. The Mongols were mostly interested in collecting tribute from the Russians and in getting fresh troops for their armies, rather than in imposing their culture on the Russians. Yet their emphasis on a very strong central authority placed its stamp on Russia and became a feature of Russian life that endured long after Mongol rule ended. Mongol rule also increased Russia's isolation from western Europe and contributed to the sense that Russians have of themselves as a combination of both east and west. The subjugation of the Russian people by the Mongol Empire became known as the Tartar (or Tatar) Yoke, after one of the Mongol groups. Today Russians have a saying, "Scratch a Russian and you'll find a Tartar." They also say, "An uninvited guest is worse than a Tartar."

In Novgorod, the Russians had to worry not only about the Mongols but about threats from the Swedes, Lithuanians, and Germans. The ruler of Novgorod, Alexander Nevsky, cooperated with the Mongols and concentrated on defeating western invasions. In a series of stunning victories, he held off their armies and is today regarded as one of the greatest Russian heroes. Novgorod, a leading center of trade featuring a humane legal system and some limited forms of representative government, finally lost status after the rise of Moscow.

People had lived on the site of the town of Moscow long before Yuri Dolgoruky built its fortification in the twelfth century, but it became an important center in the fourteenth century under such rulers as Ivan "Moneybags" Kalita, who greatly increased the size of the territory controlled by Moscow and made it the religious center of Russia. Another Moscow ruler, Dmitry Donskoy, scored the first victory over the weakening Mongol Empire at the battle of Kulikovo in 1380, which gave the Russians hope that eventually the Mongols could be expelled. Russia finally escaped from the Tartar yoke in 1480, during the rule of Ivan III, or Ivan the Great. Ivan extended Moscow's control over Novgorod and other areas and began to call himself autocrat and tsar (czar), which comes from the word Caesar, after the Roman rulers. After his marriage to a Byzantine princess from Constantinople, Ivan adopted the Byzantine two-headed eagle as his symbol. From this point on, Russia was a relatively unified state with Moscow as its chief city.

Ivan the Great's grandson, Ivan IV, known as Ivan the Terrible, was the first ruler to have himself crowned tsar of Russia. Ivan called together the *zemsky sobor*, or country council, an advisory group representing various social groups, such as the church, tradespeople, and landlords. This provided some input of opinion from the people and gave some support to legal and governmental reforms.

During Ivan's reign, the nobility, the *boyars*, came under much tighter control of the tsar, who required their support of his army. He reformed and strengthened the military, which was soon engaged in a struggle with the Tartars to the east and south. In a great victory, the Russian army captured the Tartar capital at Kazan on the Volga River, then moved south to take Astrakhan. The most famous and beautiful building in Russia, St. Basil's Cathedral on Red Square, was erected to commemorate the victory at Kazan.

Ivan suffered violent mood swings and could be exceptionally cruel. He became increasingly suspicious of his boyars and even his advisors. He set up a special group called the *oprichnina* to exterminate anyone who crossed him. This band of men, dressed in black, brought a reign of terror to Russia. Ivan's violence reached a peak when he struck his oldest son and heir Ivan a mortal blow with a pointed staff shortly before his own death.

Ivan's reign saw the increase of the tsar's power at the expense not only of the nobility, but also of the peasants, who became more closely tied to the land. His reign also saw reforms and the expansion of Russia, including even a brief penetration beyond the Ural Mountains into Siberia. Relations with western Europe increased as England opened up a trade route to the north through Archangel, particularly important after Ivan lost his access to the Baltic in battles in that area. It would be left to Peter I to permanently open up a window to the West on the Baltic Sea.

Ivan was succeeded by his oldest surviving son Fyodor, at whose death Boris Godunov, Fyodor's brother-in-law, was chosen to rule, because Ivan's third son, Dmitry, had died during his brother's short reign, and there was no direct heir. An impostor, a False Dmitry, suddenly invaded with Polish troops and claimed the throne, gaining it in fact when Boris suddenly died. When False Dmitry was killed by the boyars, he was replaced by a second False Dmitry and other pretenders to the throne. During this time, a boyar, Vasily Shuisky, sat on the throne for a short time, and for a while Polish invaders ruled. Everywhere there was turmoil, and the entire period from 1604 to 1613 became known as the Time of Troubles. Finally the Russians united to expel the Poles, bringing an end to this turbulent time. Instrumental in liberating Russia were a butcher, Kuzma Minin, who inspired an effort to form a militia, and Dmitry Pozharsky, a nobleman who commanded a force that freed Moscow. A statue to them can be found on Red Square.

In 1613, the zemsky sobor elected a grand-nephew of Ivan IV's wife as tsar, because there was no clear heir to the throne. Mikhail Romanov, who was still in his teens when he ascended the throne, did not prove to be a very effective ruler, and he is mostly remembered as the first of the Romanov dynasty that ruled Russia until the monarchy was toppled during the Russian revolution of 1917.

The seventeenth century saw a decline in the power of the zemsky sobor and a growth of centralized power at the expense of not only the nobles and merchants, but the Russian Orthodox Church, peasants, and townspeople. The Orthodox Church, under the leadership of Nikon, attempted to increase its own power and autonomy, but eventually the tsar moved against Nikon and took steps to ensure the primacy of the state over the church. The peasants, who made up most of the population, found their position worse than ever. Once free to move about, the peasants had their movements more and more restricted until in 1649 they found themselves bound to the bit of land on which they were now officially registered by the government. In the towns, people became unhappy with taxes and the debasement of coinage.

There were uprisings in the towns, but the most famous uprising was that led by the Cossack Stenka Razin in the area of the Volga and Don rivers.

Stenka Razin, who stirred thousands of peasants to join his army to seek freedom, was captured and brutally executed. Today he is remembered as a folk hero.

Despite a troubled economy and inefficient army, Russia's territory expanded greatly during the seventeenth century. After a long struggle with Poland, Russia gained control of part of Ukraine in the west. In the east, Russia pushed over the Urals into Siberia and all the way to the Pacific. Hunters and fur traders moved farther and farther east, seeking the beautiful, glossy pelts of Siberian animals. Russians also began mining and farming in these areas. As they moved eastward, the Russians encountered little resistance from the various native Siberian tribes, but after some problems with China, the government did find it necessary to conclude a border treaty defining the frontier.

PETER THE GREAT AND CATHERINE THE GREAT

Peter I, known in the West as Peter the Great, the most famous of all Russian tsars, ascended to the throne at the age of ten in 1682. He shared the throne with his weak-minded brother for four years, but the real ruler during the early period was his sister Sofia. During his teen years, Peter developed an interest in the military and formed two regiments that later became the Preobrazhensky and Semyonovsky guards. He also made friends among foreigners living in Russia and learned a lot from them, including European techniques of shipbuilding. He developed an appreciation for Western technology and culture that would lead to a huge influx of European ideas into Russia during his reign.

Much of Peter's time was spent in military campaigns to protect Russia and extend Russia's access to the sea. He built a navy and seized the Turkish fort at Azov in the south as a step toward opening up that area to Russian domination. To gain allies against Turkey, Peter decided to travel with a group of his advisors to western Europe to drum up support and to learn as much as he could about European life. He spent over a year in Europe, actually working as a shipbuilder in Holland and visiting shipyards in England as well. Exceptionally tall and very striking in appearance, he made an impression wherever he went. He was curious about everything and wanted to try doing everything himself. During his travels, he persuaded hundreds of craftsmen and technicians to travel to Russia to teach Russians how to do what he had seen in Europe.

Forced to return to Russia to deal with an uprising of Sofia's supporters, Peter crushed them ruthlessly, and then set about instituting European customs despite great resistance. For example, he decreed that nobles had to wear Western dress and shave their beards (or pay a tax). He also decreed that noblewomen were to mingle socially with men, which had not been their custom earlier. Those opposed to the changes grumbled and called Peter the Antichrist, for they felt his changes violated the Orthodox religion.

Peter's attempt to line up allies against Turkey was unsuccessful, and he turned his attention toward getting sea access in the north instead of the south, in the Baltic instead of in the Black Sea. The chief threat in the north was Sweden, ruled by his capable adversary Charles XII. Peter was defeated at Narva in 1701, but finally scored an important victory over Charles at Poltava in 1709, which consolidated Russia's hold on Ukraine and access to the Baltic Sea. Peter also wrested access to the Caspian from the Persians, although he was to lose Azov again to the Turks.

His other achievements were no less impressive, if not always welcome. Besides introducing European technical skills and social customs and reforming the army and building a navy, he made the central government more efficient by setting up administrative units to help run the different branches. He brought the church under stricter government control. In the area of education, Peter encouraged the founding of schools and sent many Russians abroad to study. He laid the foundation for what would become the world-famous Academy of Sciences. To bring Russia more in line with Europe, he even paid attention to small matters like calendar reform, so that the Russian year would begin at the same time as Europe's, rather than in September, and the years would bear the same numbers.

Peter's best-known achievement is undoubtedly the founding of the city, his "window on the West," St. Petersburg, which he named for his patron saint. Founded in 1703, St. Petersburg became the capital in 1712. Built on marshy mosquito-infested land at the mouth of the Neva River, the city claimed the lives of thousands of workers during its construction. Among the earliest buildings were Peter's own small house and the Peter and Paul fortress. Peter envisioned a great stone city, and to that end decreed that for the time being all stone construction in Russia be concentrated in St. Petersburg, where he had imported foreign architects to help plan the new city. By the end of Peter's reign in 1725, St. Petersburg was already a beautiful capital with impressive buildings lining long straight wide streets, among them the Nevsky Prospect, the most famous street in Russia.

After Peter's reign, Russia would never be the same. The eighteenth century saw a continuation of increased relations with the West. Peter was succeeded by a series of rulers over the next four decades, most notably by two women, Anna and Elizabeth, but the next great ruler was Catherine II, Catherine the Great, herself not a Russian, but a German princess who began her reign in 1762 when her husband, Peter III, was overthrown in a coup. A highly intelligent, artistic, and cultivated person, Catherine conducted a brilliant court life and encouraged adoption of many aspects of Western art and culture into Russian upper-class life, laying the groundwork for the flowering of Russian culture in such areas as literature, music, and ballet in the next century.

Catherine's reign saw the expansion of Russia into Poland and into the area around the Black Sea, including the Crimea. Internally, her achievements were mixed. On the positive side, she made advances in the areas of education and health, building schools and extending education to women, erecting hospitals, and encouraging smallpox vaccination. However, most Russians continued to lead bleak lives as serfs tied to the land, and their lot actually worsened during Catherine's reign. Unrest among the Cossacks led to a general uprising in 1772. The rumor spread that Peter III was not dead and that the Cossack leader Emelyan Pugachev was actually Peter. The peasants joined the Cossacks in forming an army, but the government was ultimately victorious, executing Pugachev and strengthening the authority of the nobility over the peasants.

FROM NAPOLEON TO REVOLUTION

The short reign of Catherine's son Paul I was followed by that of Alexander I, who became tsar in 1801. The main event of this period was Napoleon's invasion of Russia in 1812. Napoleon entered Russia with a huge army of hundreds of thousands of soldiers, most of whom perished in the winter snows as they retreated from Moscow. Napoleon's invasion was vividly described in Leo Tolstoy's great novel titled *War and Peace*.

When Alexander died suddenly in 1825, there was some uncertainty about the succession, because Constantine, Alexander's closest heir, was unwilling to rule and had given way to his brother Nicholas. During this time of confusion, revolutionaries pressed for rule by Constantine—and a constitution—in an action that became known as the Decembrist Revolt. Some of the revolutionaries were executed, and others were exiled to Siberia. When Nicholas ascended the throne, he became one of the most repressive tsars of the period, attempting to keep tight control over any signs of unrest. Through control of educational institutions, censorship, travel restrictions, and brutal suppression of revolutionary groups, Nicholas prevented any major uprisings, although there were hundreds of minor revolts.

Concerned about the future of Russia and about what the path of the nation's development should be, intellectuals were divided roughly into two camps, which became known as the Slavophiles and the Westernizers. The Slavophiles were more conservative and praised the traditional Russian values and religion before the time of Peter I. The Westernizers emphasized the benefits of adopting European methods and ideas.

Writers were swept up into the political discussions and suffered the consequences. Among the writers who chafed under the restrictions placed on them by the tsarist regime were Alexander Pushkin and Fyodor Dostoevsky. Pushkin had his travel restricted and suffered exile from the capital; his works were closely monitored by the tsar himself. For his political activity, Dostoevsky was arrested and sent to prison in Siberia during this time.

Russia continued to expand under Nicholas, this time gaining land to the south near the Black Sea. Tensions in this area led to the Crimean War toward the end of Nicholas's reign. The British and French sided with the Turks, leading to a Russian defeat.

The new tsar, Alexander II, ushered in an era of reform. The most far-reaching reform was the liberation of the serfs in 1861. A gradual improvement in the lives of the serfs had been going on for many years. By Alexander II's time, they had more control over the crops they raised and could sell them, and even buy land. Those subject to compulsory military service had the number of years of service reduced. Emancipation was the culmination of these earlier efforts to ameliorate the lives of the majority of Russians. Along with freedom, peasants were given land, although it was held not by individuals, but in common by the *mir*, the village collective.

In the 1860s, numerous other reforms were undertaken in the areas of the court system, education, censorship, and local government. Censorship became milder, and education became more widespread for both sexes. Yet many were still dissatisfied and called for more radical action. A radical group finally ended by assassinating the tsar in 1881.

Meanwhile, Russia continued to expand into Central Asia, and consolidated its hold on the Caucasus region and on parts of the Far East. Russia sold Alaska to the United States in 1867.

Alexander III's reign was much more repressive than his predecessor's. Finally, in 1894, came the reign of the last tsar, Nicholas II. Despite some great achievements like the building of the Trans-Siberian railroad, the mood in the country was volatile. Some reforms were going very slowly or had been reversed. The defeat of the Russians at the hands of the Japanese in the Russo-Japanese War in 1905 was psychologically devastating. That same year, soldiers fired on a group of workers who had marched to the palace to ask for reforms. This event, which became known as Bloody Sunday, led the tsar to agree to the formation of a parliament, called the Duma, but the unrest increased. In October 1905, there was a general strike.

Russia was ill-prepared for World War I, which broke out in August 1914. In a burst of patriotism, the name of the capital was changed to Petrograd ("Peter's City") because St. Petersburg sounded too German. However, any enthusiasm for the war against Germany was short-lived. Battles were lost, food and fuel were in short supply, morale was low, and life both on the front lines and at home was disrupted. Support for the tsar declined sharply. Nicholas II was out of touch with the mood of the country; he and his unpopular foreign wife Alexandra were under the influence of the unsavory monk Rasputin, whose help with the care of their only son, a hemophiliac, Alexandra valued.

RUSSIA UNDER COMMUNISM

In February 1917, the Russians revolted once again. Shortages of food and other supplies led to riots, which the government was unable to quell. Nicholas abdicated and the Duma set up a provisional government. At the urging of their leader, Vladimir Lenin, on October 25, 1917, the bolsheviks, a communist faction, staged a coup and seized control of key points in the capital; they eventually dominated the whole country. In the ensuing years, the October Revolution would be celebrated on November 7, after the new government abandoned the old-style calendar and adopted the more accurate one in use in the West.

The new government moved the capital back to Moscow and concluded peace with Germany. Their new flag was red with a hammer and sickle, representing the workers and peasants, and their army became known as the Red Army. The Reds did not win complete control over the country without a struggle, however. Opposition forces, known as the Whites, fought bitterly, supported minimally by anticommunist foreign governments in Europe, Japan, and the United States. Most of the upper and middle classes, including the intelligentsia, supported the Whites, while the workers supported the Reds. The peasants distrusted both, but were more inclined to support the Reds rather than side with those who had so recently held them as serfs. To ensure that Nicholas II would never regain the throne, the communists murdered him and his wife and children in 1918 in Ekaterinburg, where they were being detained. After years of struggle, the Reds finally won, inheriting a land exhausted by fighting, disease, and famine. Several million people had died and another million had emigrated. The country itself was smaller, having lost control over the Baltic region as well as other border territories

after World War I. It would be known as the Union of Soviet Socialist Republics (USSR) or Soviet Union.

Ideally, the communists would have liked to maintain control over all aspects of the economy, ostensibly in the name of the people. But a temporary retreat from that position would revitalize the economy more quickly. Lenin proposed a New Economic Policy (NEP) to inject life into the economy. Small businesses were allowed to operate, and the peasants were allowed to sell their products directly to customers for the time being. The 1920s were a time of great vitality in the culture, the decade that produced the finest, most progressive literature and art of the entire communist period.

But this heady time was not to last. Lenin, who died in 1924, and his successor Joseph Stalin, preferred to rule with an iron fist. The New Economic Policy was followed by the First Five-Year Plan in 1928 and by what was essentially a dictatorship headed by Stalin. Stalin forced the peasants to combine their farms into large state, or collective, farms, which meant the peasants would have to turn over most of what they produced to the state. This collectivization effort resulted in much hardship and suffering, including exile to prison camps or even death for the peasants, many of whom tried futilely to resist Stalin. The Five-Year Plan also provided for the rapid expansion of heavy industry. In the area of culture, Stalin began insisting that all citizens, including writers, should work toward the common goal, which meant that writers should write works that would promote the Five-Year Plan. This form of control spelled the end of the burst of avant-garde creativity in Russia, especially because it was accompanied by the threat of force.

The next decade in Russia was a nightmare. Stalin tightened the levers of control on all aspects of society, squelching creativity and bringing real fear into the lives of every Russian. Even Stalin's comrades were not safe, for his suspicious and paranoid nature led him to turn on former colleagues, as well as on anyone he perceived as opposed to his plans for the country. During the mid 1930s, Stalin conducted purges, in which untold numbers of Russians were arrested by the secret police, put on trial, and ultimately imprisoned or shot. Russia lost many of its most intelligent and talented people in this ordeal, which weakened the arts and the sciences as well as the army, not to mention wrecking the lives of millions of Russians. Hardly any family was untouched by the great terror, one of the darkest pages in all Russian history.

Russia was not well prepared for World War II. Stalin had signed a non-aggression pact with Adolf Hitler, with the idea that each could expand without threat from the other. However, in June 1941 Hitler invaded Russia anyway. Germany penetrated deep into the USSR, taking Kiev, laying siege to Leningrad (as St. Petersburg or Petrograd was now called), and pushing

on to Moscow. Russia joined forces with the Allies, including the United States after the December 1941 attack on Pearl Harbor, in an effort to repel Hitler's forces.

Russia suffered terribly during the war. Estimates of deaths range up to 27 million, including both military and civilian losses. Leningrad alone lost several hundred thousand people to starvation during the 900-day siege of that city. The city of Stalingrad (formerly Tsaritsyn, now Volgograd) on the Volga River was reduced to rubble during the winter of 1942–1943, although the battle there was a turning point for the war in Russia. Finally the Russians were able to repel the Germans and push westward across Eastern Europe into German territory. The fighting in Europe ceased in May 1945.

Despite the fact that they had been unprepared for the war, the Russians had several advantages that helped them ultimately prevail. In addition to mistakes made by the Germans and assistance from the Allies, the Russians once again had their country's sheer size and harsh winters on their side. The military fought valiantly. Both military and civilians showed great determination and bravery in their efforts to push the invaders out of their land. Despite the distaste many felt for the communist regime, the Russians showed their deep love for Mother Russia, their native soil, by defending her. The communist government helped foster that patriotism by relaxing the controls on religion and on literature during the war and by promising better times after the war. Yet not all Russians were persuaded. Some Soviet citizens, mostly those in the other republics but also some Russians, tried to undercut the regime either by not resisting the Germans or by actively helping them. At the end of the war, some chose not to return to their homes, preferring freedom in the West.

After the war, Russia maintained its grip on Eastern Europe and on the eastern part of Germany, in effect controlling these regions. East Germany, Poland, Czechoslovakia, Romania, Bulgaria, Hungary, and for a while Yugoslavia and Albania were under Soviet domination. An Iron Curtain was said to separate these countries from the free countries of Western Europe. The distrust and competition between the communist bloc in the East and the democracies of the West was called the Cold War, which persisted for forty years.

Inside Russia, Russians began to rebuild cities and industries destroyed in the war. Stalin established new Five-Year Plans directed at both the industrial and agricultural sectors. Collective farms were enlarged and consolidated. Heavy industry was emphasized over consumer goods, although the standard of living for individual citizens did improve. But once again Stalin clamped down on those he felt might oppose him, arresting and imprisoning them.

FROM KHRUSHCHEV TO PUTIN

A new era began after Stalin's death in 1953. After a period of shared leadership and of jockeying for power, Nikita Khrushchev emerged as the new leader of Russia. He denounced Stalin at the Twentieth Party Congress in 1956, accusing him of being a cruel tyrant who was responsible both for the killing of innocent people during the purges and for neglecting to prepare Russia for World War II. Eventually, Stalin's body, which lay beside Lenin's in a tomb on Red Square, was removed and buried separately. Stalingrad was renamed Volgograd, and other traces of Stalin's "cult of personality" were erased from the scene.

A new era seemed to dawn in Russia as it became clear that Stalin's terror was finally over. A "thaw" occurred, during which time a little more freedom of expression was allowed. Some cultural exchanges were made, and Khrushchev himself visited the West. Russia made advances in the field of space, launching the first satellite, Sputnik, in 1957 and then putting the first human, Yuri Gagarin, in space in 1961. Nonetheless, improvements in the standard of living of ordinary Russians lagged behind, and agricultural shortages were frequent.

Trouble arose in Eastern Europe, particularly in Hungary, where Russia crushed a revolution in 1956. Five years later, China and Russia essentially parted ways, dividing the communist world. Russia continued to try to expand its influence, however, even into the western hemisphere. By 1962, Khrushchev had established missile bases only ninety miles off American shores in Cuba. War was averted when Khrushchev agreed to demands that the bases be removed.

Khrushchev fell from power in 1964. The following period, dominated primarily by Leonid Brezhnev, became known as the years of stagnation. Although there were improvements, the standard of living remained behind that in the West. Agriculture remained a big problem area, even necessitating the import of wheat from America. Trade with the West increased, and tensions abated somewhat with the arms agreements reached as a result of the Strategic Arms Limitation Talks (SALT).

Throughout this period there were problems between East and West, however, as Russia and the West both sought influence in Africa, Asia, and other areas. Unrest continued in East Europe. Even in Russia itself, some citizens clamored to leave. Hundreds of thousands of Jews were allowed to emigrate, many of them settling in Israel or the United States. Outspoken critics of Russia still faced danger. Some were imprisoned or hospitalized or even forcibly exiled, including some well-known writers.

After the death of Brezhnev in 1982, the next major leader was Mikhail Gorbachev, who came to power in 1985. Gorbachev's era popularized two terms, *perestroika*, or rebuilding, and *glasnost*, or openness. Perestroika was envisioned as regenerating the Soviet economy through increased productivity and modernization of equipment, but within the framework of communism. One effort to improve productivity was the disastrous effort to cut alcohol consumption, which only led to the illegal production of alcohol. Glasnost meant that people could more openly discuss the problems that faced Russia and led to an outpouring of literature, both new works and works that had been long forbidden. Meanwhile problems faced the country as Russia fought an unpopular war in Afghanistan and as unrest increased in Eastern Europe. The fallout from a nuclear disaster at Chernobyl pointed up the poor condition of much of Russia's infrastructure and the precarious state of the environment after decades of abuse. Finally matters came to a head when communist regimes fell in Eastern Europe and republics within the Soviet Union itself demanded their autonomy. The three Baltic republics—Estonia, Latvia, and Lithuania—were determined to become independent countries. In the south, there were rumblings in Georgia, Armenia, and Azerbaijan. Alternate attempts to placate or crush these and other stirrings within the Soviet Union were not successful. With regard to the spectacular collapse of communism in Eastern Europe in 1989 and the reunification of Germany, Russia's reaction was much more restrained, to the point that Gorbachev was awarded the Nobel Prize for peace in 1990.

Gorbachev's days in power were numbered. While Gorbachev was out of Moscow in 1991, a disgruntled group of communists staged a coup. On August 19, it was announced that Gorbachev had resigned. Soldiers and tanks were brought in to support the coup but the conspirators were loath to engage in any real violence, and it was soon clear that the soldiers had no intention of firing on their own people in any case. The coup ultimately failed because it lacked the support it needed from the army, key leaders, and the population at large. The head of the Russian republic, Boris Yeltsin, vigorously opposed the coup, and emerged as a hero for saving Gorbachev's position. The morning of the coup, Yeltsin went to the Russian Supreme Soviet building, known as the White House, which his supporters had surrounded with barricades of trucks, buses, wire, and debris. In a dramatic gesture, he came out and stood on an armored vehicle, defying the communists who were seeking to unseat Gorbachev. The situation was tense for the next few days, but finally the coup collapsed. When Gorbachev returned, it was Yeltsin who won the people's affection, and within a short time, Gorbachev had to yield his po-

sition as head of state to Yeltsin. In December 1991, the Soviet Union dissolved, and a new Commonwealth of Independent States was formed.

The mood was euphoric for a short time as Yeltsin began the process of dismantling the communist system and replacing it with a capitalist economy within a democratic country. That mood soon dissipated as the economy deteriorated. Hostility between the new parliament, again called the Duma, and Yeltsin broke into open conflict as Duma supporters took over the Moscow mayor's office and tried to take the television center at Ostankino in Moscow. The conflict ended after the army, in support of Yeltsin, was able to take the White House where the Duma met. Within months the opposition leaders were pardoned. A new constitution gave Yeltsin more power, while guaranteeing free enterprise and individual freedoms. In 1994–1996, Yeltsin attempted without much success to crush a move for independence in a southern region called Chechnya. Yeltsin won reelection in 1996. Two years later the country was again in crisis as the government defaulted on some debts, and the national currency, the ruble, fell in value. The Duma tried to impeach Yeltsin in 1999, but he had no trouble defeating the attempt to oust him. Yeltsin changed prime ministers with increasing frequency and in 1999 named Vladimir Putin to the post. Putin's popularity soared when he spoke harshly about taking revenge on the Chechens, who were blamed for several apartment building bombings. The Russian army again went into Chechnya, this time determined to win. The war, which devastated much of Chechnya, including the major city of Grozny, was popular with Russians who were demoralized with the economic situation and their loss of status in the world community.

At the very end of 1999, Yeltsin stunned the world with the announcement that he was retiring several months before his term was to expire. He appointed Putin in his place, with elections to be held in March 2000, thus giving Putin an undoubted edge against any competitors for the post. In his farewell speech, he expressed satisfaction with the recent Duma elections and felt that his work was done, that Russia would now never return to the past. In a moving conclusion, he asked forgiveness that he was unable to bring the people easily to the bright future they all hoped for.

Although Yeltsin's popularity was very low as he left office, like Gorbachev's before him, both men will probably have their reputations reevaluated by future generations of Russians. Gorbachev tried with some success to bring freedom and openness to Russia within the communist system. Yeltsin continued his work, creating and preserving an infant democracy with freedom of the press and freedom of speech and a flawed but functioning capitalist economic system. Under the guidance of these two men, Russia at last entered the free world. Despite the dire situation in Russia today, that is no mean accomplishment.

MODERN RUSSIA

Russia faced enormous problems in the 1990s. After seventy years of communism, with its planned economy and controlled currency, Russia was ill-equipped for a rapid conversion to capitalism. Factories were in poor repair and inefficient, and their consumer products were shoddy. Managers did not have the know-how to function in a market economy, nor were workers prepared for the uncertainties of the marketplace. The transportation and delivery system for the goods they produced was poor. Crime bosses became rich as protection money was extorted from businesses. Skyrocketing inflation proved devastating, especially for people on pensions. It was not unusual for people to go months with no pay, or to receive pay in the form of consumer products like vodka or even tombstones. Foreign firms opened branches in Russia, but many pulled out again, discouraged by the crime and the lack of government cooperation and protection. Foreign entrepreneurs, initially excited by the opportunities Russia offered, also became discouraged. The international community poured money into Russia, but wanted assurances that the money was not being skimmed off by corrupt officials or diverted by criminals, as was sometimes the case. In 1998, the ruble, already considerably devalued, suddenly plunged to a new low, shaking confidence even further. Women in particular suffered in the new Russia, as age-old prejudice, no longer checked by communist ideology, caused many women to be eased out of good jobs and replaced by men. As the century drew to a close, Russia continued to flounder economically.

The military was another area of concern. As soldiers were pulled out of Eastern Europe, Russia needed to house them and pay them, both troublesome propositions. Morale was low and preparedness suffered. Equipment of all sorts was poorly maintained. Internal disturbances, like the push for independence in Chechnya, still called for military intervention. The weakness of Russia's military was quite apparent as the army tried to defeat the Chechen rebels in two separate periods of conflict. Another concern was the aging nuclear strike force. The Y2K computer problem, which Russia was slow in addressing, made the people of the world worry that Russian missiles might accidentally be fired. As it was, several locations were threatened by nuclear contamination from leakages. The West also worried as Russia, strapped for cash, made overtures to sell its weapons and planes to other countries. The space program, once the pride of every Russian, limped into the new century, its glorious but aging space station Mir, already aloft fourteen years, and its participation in the international space station problematic because of the poor economy.

There were health issues as well. The environment, suffering from years of abuse, continued to be threatened by dirty factory emissions. Forests were heavily logged, with little regard for the future. Heavy alcohol consumption, especially by men, contributed toward a rising mortality rate unprecedented in modern industrial nations. Diseases such as diphtheria reappeared, and the incidence of AIDS and other sexually transmitted diseases increased. Hospital conditions were deplorable, and a lack of medical supplies was a common condition. Nutrition suffered as the result of crop failures and transportation problems, as well as inflation. Not only was the population as a whole shrinking, but the children of the new generation were growing up shorter and smaller than the previous generation.

Various factions struggled for control of the hearts and minds of Russians. The old communists managed to keep a high profile in the government, while groups of various other persuasions, even including monarchists, vied for attention. While attempting to build a future, or at least get through the shaky present, Russians began the long process of coming to terms with their recent past. Muscovites took down the statue of Felix Dzerzhinsky, founder and former head of the secret police, and then discussed putting it up again. They debated whether to take Lenin out of his glass case in the tomb on Red Square and bury him. They paid honor to the bones of Nicholas II and his family, interring the bodies (two were still missing) in St. Petersburg, which they were no longer calling Leningrad. At the beginning of the decade, many cities and streets and institutions, renamed after communist leaders, reverted to their prerevolutionary names. Later this tendency leveled off, with the result that today there is a mix of prerevolutionary and communist labels.

Religion was another area of concern. The communist regime had promoted atheism. After the fall of communism, many people wanted to return to the days when Russian Orthodoxy was the prevailing religion. However, in addition to many domestic religious groups of various stripes, there were groups from outside Russia that sought new converts, and many Russians were interested in the occult, astrology, and the paranormal.

The question of what was "Russian" was debated. Some parts of the former Soviet Union, the Russian empire, emphatically wanted nothing to do with Russia, while others wanted to maintain some sort of close economic or military relationship. Even within Russia, the largest of the fifteen republics in the old Soviet Union, some areas wanted autonomy and were willing to fight to get it. Additionally, in the parts of the Russian republic that did not want independence, there were different nationalities and religions that were neither ethnically Russian nor Russian Orthodox. The terms *russky* and *rossiisky* were used to define Russians: russky meant ethnically Russian, and rossiisky simply meant part of the old Russian republic and was more inclusive.

In the early heady days of freedom, many wanted to open the door more widely to the West, to Europe and more particularly to America: American clothes, food, music, American everything was popular. Like English, the Russian language has always been hospitable to new vocabulary and American-English words flooded into Russia by the hundreds. "Kompyuter," "printer," "faks" (fax), "kseroks" (xerox), "menedzher" (manager), and "Pitstsa Hat" (Pizza Hut) became familiar to Russians, who already knew "Kokakola" and "Pepsi." Inevitably, there was a backlash, as those who wanted to return to their own Russian roots, rather than borrow from the West, began to question using America as a role model. Suspicion of American motives and questioning of American values entered the dialogue. Anti-American feeling grew particularly intense after the NATO bombing of Russia's longtime ally Yugoslavia. Once again, as so often in the past, Russians weighed what was good to preserve from their own heritage with what might profitably be borrowed from the West. As they entered the new century, nothing was certain.

SUGGESTED READINGS

Brown, Archie, Michael Kaser, and Gerald S. Smith, eds. *The Cambridge Encyclopedia of Russia and the Former Soviet Union.* Cambridge: Cambridge University Press, 1994.

Mackenzie, David, and Michael W. Curran. *A History of Russia, the Soviet Union, and Beyond.* Belmont, CA: Wadsworth, 1998.

Riasanovsky, Nicholas V. *A History of Russia.* New York: Oxford University Press, 1993.

Service, Robert. *A History of Twentieth-Century Russia.* Cambridge: Harvard University Press, 1997.

Zenkovsky, Serge A., ed. *Medieval Russia's Epics, Chronicles, and Tales.* New York: Dutton, 1974.

Where to begin on the Internet:

Bucknell Russian Studies Department. www.departments.bucknell.edu/russian

CIA World Factbooks. www.odci.gov/cia/publications/factbook/rs.html

Russian Life magazine. www.rispubs.com/rltop10.cfm

2

Thought and Religion

WHEN THE SOVIET UNION dissolved in 1991, Russians followed a familiar pattern in their history. Needing a model for the future, they looked in two directions: outward toward other countries, in particular the West, and inward toward their own roots. The Russians were searching not so much for an economic model, although that was important to them, as for a spiritual model, a way to "be." This was not the first time they had faced the choice of following their own way, adopting foreign ways, or, inevitably, of finding some combination of the two that suited them.

Deep in the past, Russians had been pagan, worshiping old gods such as Perun, Dazhbog, Khors, Simargl, Stribog, and Mokosh, whose idols Prince Vladimir erected in the capital city of Kiev in the year 980. The principal god was Perun, a god whose symbol was an ax. Dazhbog and Khors were sun gods. Mokosh was a female, who may have been associated with the idea of Mother Earth. People continued to believe in these and other old gods long after Russia became Christian and pagan rituals became intertwined with Christian ones: some ancient traditions survived into the early twentieth century. The largely agrarian peasant population held firmly to several rituals connected with the earth itself, which they called Mother Damp Earth. The peasants reportedly sealed oaths by swallowing dirt and even asked the earth's forgiveness before death. The idea of the land, the earth, as female, is still seen in the expressions "mother-native land" and "Mother Russia." Peasants also believed in a house-spirit, the *domovoi*, as well as in spirits inhabiting the forest and the water, the *leshii* and the *rusalka* and the *vodianoi*.

Despite the strength of the old customs and beliefs, Russia also eventually embraced Christianity, an import from outside, so firmly that the country was sometimes referred to as Holy Russia. The same Vladimir who erected idols at Kiev soon thereafter converted to Christianity, following the example of his grandmother Olga. According to the old *Primary Chronicle*, the Bulgarians, Germans, Jews, and Greeks had all been urging him to adopt their various religions, and Vladimir sent emissaries out among them to see which religion was best. The emissaries reported only sorrow and stench in the Bulgarian mosques. They found no glory in the German churches. In the Byzantine Greek churches, however, they were so impressed by the splendor and beauty of the buildings and the services that they did not know whether they were on earth or in heaven. After Vladimir received signs that the Greek Church was the one he should adopt, he was baptized and married the sister of the Byzantine rulers. He ordered the statue of Perun to be tied to a horse's tail and dragged to the Dnieper River, beaten with sticks, and thrown in. He then ordered everyone to come down to the river to be baptized or risk his displeasure. Everyone waded into the river, some adults holding the children in their arms, while priests offered prayers on shore. Vladimir built churches where the idols had once stood and invited inhabitants in surrounding towns to embrace his religion. Thus Russia became Christian in the year 988.

The early church distinguished itself by its care for the poor and by its mercy: Kiev had no death penalty and did not torture people. The concept of nonresistance to evil was also important, as shown in the history of Boris and Gleb, two princes who passively submitted to their brother's attempt to have them murdered.

The years after Kiev fell to the Mongols were difficult, but the church persisted and spread. In the fourteenth century, Russia's greatest national saint, Sergey of Radonezh, founded a monastery dedicated to the Trinity at Sergiev Posad northeast of Moscow. This became the greatest religious center in Russia. Sergey inspired his adherents to spread the faith to other areas. Under his influence, Russia enjoyed the Golden Age of Russian Spirituality, which lasted from 1350 to 1550. This was also the period when the finest icons, religious pictures on wood, were painted by Andrey Rublev.

In 1054, a major split between the eastern and western portions of the Christian Church had resulted in two branches: Catholicism based in Rome and Eastern Orthodoxy based in Constantinople. Russia belonged to the eastern branch. When Constantinople fell in 1453, Russia saw herself as the new center of Christianity, the Third Rome, the first two having been Rome and Constantinople. When Ivan III, or Ivan the Great, married the niece of the Byzantine ruler and assumed the title of tsar, he reinforced the links with the previous two "Romes."

The Russian church was internally torn by conflicting values. One school of thought, represented by Nil Sorsky, said that monks should be poor and spend their time in prayer, while others, headed by Joseph of Volokolamsk, wanted a rich, activist church. They disagreed on the policy toward heretics, Nil advocating tolerance. For the time being, Joseph's group triumphed.

The relationship between church and state was also problematical. Basil the Blessed, a *yurodivy*, or fool in Christ, who renounced everything (possessions, clothes, even treasures of the mind like knowledge and rationality) to serve Christ, was honored by Ivan IV (the Terrible), who accepted criticism from him which he would not tolerate from one not so blessed. The famous St. Basil's Cathedral in Moscow is named for him. In the next century, the 1600s, the patriarch Nikon wanted not just honor from the tsar, he wanted the church supreme over the state. Nikon had grand plans for the church. Russians were very concerned with ritual and tradition and liked to do everything the same from generation to generation, stressing the continuity within the church. Nikon wanted to reform these rituals to bring them more in line with what the modern Greeks were doing. This meant making a few alterations in the sacred books and changing the way Russians crossed themselves. Many people balked at being forced to cross themselves with three fingers instead of two the way their ancestors had always done. Those who refused to change were cruelly punished, imprisoned, or even burned. Avvakum, one of those Old Believers, left an autobiography which is still compelling to read hundreds of years later. The schism in the Russian church never healed, and there are still Old Believers in Russia to this day. Peter I, the Great, far from accepting the idea of a supreme church, would eventually put it under state supervision, abolishing the office of patriarch and appointing a twelve-person synod to govern it and limiting the church's activities in other ways. Peter was determined that Russia was to become westernized, and a powerful church did not fit in with his plans.

The eighteenth century continued the process of westernization, but in the nineteenth, the debate over foreign ideas and domestic traditions once again came to the fore. Two schools of thought arose, the Slavophiles and the Westernizers. The Slavophiles admired Russian culture and traditions, praising "Orthodoxy, Autocracy, and Nationalism." The primacy of the Orthodox Church was central to their ideas, although they were also interested in closer ties with other Slavic lands which were not Orthodox. They were uninterested in adopting Western forms of government, believing that the *mir*, the peasant commune, was a true form of self-government within the autocratic regime headed by the tsar. They did want the serfs liberated, which occurred in 1861, but did not see any need for a parliamentary democracy. They stressed the spiritual nature of the Russian people, who should not find it necessary to look to the West for guidance.

Chief among the Slavophile thinkers were Ivan Kireevsky and Alexey Khomyakov, both of whom placed Orthodox Christianity at the center of their thought. Khomyakov developed the important concept of *sobornost*, which refers to the free community of people unified by their love of the same values. Slavophiles might appreciate some aspects of the West, but on the whole, to them Europeans seemed too materialistic and less in touch with the spiritual life. Slavophiles thought that Russians were at least on a par with European culture and perhaps were superior.

Westernizers were more skeptical of the value of Russian traditions and wanted to modernize Russian institutions along the lines of Western Europe. They felt that during the two centuries of domination by the Mongols, ending in 1480, Russia had fallen behind, missed the Renaissance, and never caught up. They were more concerned with political reform, on the model of Western societies, than they were with Russia's mission or her church. Some Westernizers wanted a constitutional monarchy while others leaned toward socialism of one form or another. Westernizers were influenced, as might be expected, by European philosophers of the time. Among the best-known Westernizers were Alexander Herzen, who founded the first Russian free press (abroad) and Vissarion Belinsky, Russia's leading literary critic.

Among the more radical nineteenth-century thinkers were Mikhail Bakunin, Nikolai Chernyshevsky, and Dmitry Pisarev. Bakunin was early under the influence of the German philosopher Hegel, but later turned to activism. He thought that revolution, which he saw as good, justified any methods necessary to achieve it. Chernyshevsky believed that science could answer all questions, and he advocated socialism. Pisarev was a nihilist and a utilitarian, who thought that a pair of boots was worth more than a play by Shakespeare. Finally came the Populists, utopian socialists who thought that the peasants would be the class that would lead to revolution.

Russian writers got caught up in the debate over Russia's future. Nikolai Gogol wrote about Russia's mission in the world and was closely aligned with Slavophile thinking. Ivan Turgenev wrote about social problems in his novels from a Westernizer standpoint. In his writings, Leo Tolstoy dealt with social questions such as women's role in the modern world and education. In his later life, he turned to religious writing, retranslating and interpreting the Bible, earning the displeasure of the church and eventually excommunication. The ideas of nonresistance to evil and nonviolence were central to his thinking. Dostoevsky's novels are deeply concerned with Christian ideas of sin, suffering, forgiveness, and salvation. Both Tolstoy and Dostoevsky were regarded by contemporaries as conservatives, although a closer reading reveals some very profound and radical ideas. Both were interested in the resurgence of religion in Russia, marked by the founding of many new monasteries. This was also the time of the *startsy*, or elders, whose center was at the Optino hermitage, but whose influence on a revival of monasticism spread across Russia. Dostoevsky's character Zosima in *The Brothers Karamazov* is based on the startsy.

Toward the end of the century, Russians became interested in mysticism and the occult. Systems of thought like Freemasonry and Theosophy, and later Anthroposophy, became popular. This was the time of the great religious philosopher and mystic, Vladimir Solovyov. Solovyov had visions of the Divine Sophia, the female incarnation of wisdom. From the times of Mother Damp Earth, Russians had made the female a central figure in their religion. In Christianity, they exalted the figure of Mary, whom they revered less in her aspect as virgin than in her role as mother, all-merciful and all-forgiving. In his philosophy, Solovyov used the female Sophia as a symbol of the unity of the universe. He thought that love was a way for humans to strive toward unity. Solovyov's philosophy and imagery had a great influence both on later religious thinkers and on Symbolist writers.

POSTREVOLUTION

On the eve of the 1917 revolution, some Russians sensed a huge change was near, perhaps the second coming of Christ, perhaps the dawn of a radiant future, democratic or socialist or communist, perhaps the end of all things, or perhaps the coming of the Antichrist. As it turned out, the communist state that arose from the rubble of revolution and civil war proved hostile to all forms of thought other than those of its own system, which was based on the works of Karl Marx and modified by others, including the Russian leader Vladimir Lenin. For more than half a century, Marxism-Leninism prevailed in Russia. Openly professing other systems of thought was decidedly risky. The Marxist-Leninist system held that there was an economic basis to society, that capitalism would give way to communism in a class struggle between the privileged classes and the proletarian and peasant classes, and that the transition would be led by a strong Communist Party in control of the state. The state was essentially atheist, although it took on some traditional trappings of religion, especially in its treatment of Lenin's body after his death in 1924. His body was preserved and displayed on public view, like Russian saints whose bodies were also displayed. People stood in line to see Lenin's body, as was the custom with the bodies of certain holy figures like Sergey of Radonezh. Lenin was depicted in children's books as loving little children, just as books showed Jesus and little children. Banners proclaimed that Lenin "lived, lives, and will live," just as might be said about Christ. He became a kind of combination George Washington and Jesus Christ figure.

Religion never died out in communist Russia, although it underwent difficult times. The communist regime was militantly atheistic and determined to tightly control any competition for the allegiance of the people, especially the church that had been so closely allied with the tsarist regime and was regarded as an oppressor. The church was stripped of most of its land, and monks were evicted from the monasteries. Many churches were closed down, stripped of their valuables, or even demolished. Shrines with relics were broken open, and precious metal ornaments were melted down. Some churches remained open and services were held, but other church activities such as charitable work and Sunday schools and study groups were not allowed. St. Basil's Cathedral became a museum. Kazan Cathedral in Leningrad (St. Petersburg) became a museum devoted to showing the atrocities committed in the name of religion. Atheism was promoted in the schools. Many priests and nuns and other church officials were persecuted, sent to camps, or imprisoned. When the Orthodox Church cooperated in opposing the Germans in World War II, Stalin allowed thousands of churches to reopen, although many would close again under later communist rulers.

Seventy years of communism had done its work. When communism finally fell in 1991, much of the population no longer believed in God and did not attend church. The people seemed to feel a hunger for some kind of spiritual life, however. Despite the fact that the country was poor and needed all its resources just to get on its feet, the Russians decided as one of their first acts to rebuild the Cathedral of Christ Savior, a huge nineteenth-century Moscow church commemorating the victory over Napoleon in 1812, which the communists under Stalin had demolished in 1931 to make way for a massive Palace of Soviets, taller than the Empire State Building and topped with a statue of Lenin larger than the Statue of Liberty. The Palace could not be completed because of the swampy ground under it, to the grim delight of the faithful, and eventually a swimming pool was put there. Now the cathedral would once again stand, commemorating not only the victory over Napoleon but a victory over Stalinist times. The Russians also rebuilt the Cathedral of Our Lady of Kazan on Red Square, which was pulled down by Stalin in 1936. Many seemed to feel that a spiritual revival, in the form of rebuilt churches, was essential to a revival in other areas, such as the economy and social conditions.

The Orthodox Church was freed to teach religion, conduct social work, and own churches once again. It rapidly began to increase the numbers of dioceses, monasteries, and seminaries; set up Sunday schools; and in general tried to regain some of its lost position in Russian life. In 1993, the church set up a university, which offers a rigorous academic program in a variety of fields, including economics, law, ecology, and languages. Students must study religion, but are not required to attend church services.

The Orthodox Church was poised to fill the void in people's lives, but it had a lot of problems and a lot of competition. The church itself was poor. Many churches were in bad condition and needed repairs. Monasteries all over Russia were in shambles. There were not enough priests to go around and even the ones they had needed new training. There were factions within the church. The Orthodox Russians who had emigrated to the West at the time of the revolution were leery of the church in Russia, which some regarded as having compromised too much with the communists. Inside Russia, Orthodox factions disagreed on which groups should get control of the limited resources and what their position should be on issues like anti-Semitism. One group, Pamiat (which means "memory"), was openly anti-Semitic and very nationalistic, while other groups were more moderate. Another group, the Free Orthodox Church in Suzdal, did not want to be under the control of the regular Orthodox Church. A group of Ukrainian Catholics who had been merged with the Orthodox Church under the communists now wanted to break away. Then there were the Old Believers, who did not form a coherent group, but belonged to several splinter groups.

As if that were not enough trouble for the Orthodox Church, there was competition from other churches. Evangelical groups, usually referred to as Baptists, had long been active in Russia and had suffered under both the tsarist regime and the communists. The writer Alexander Solzhenitsyn drew a memorable portrait of a Baptist named Alyoshka in a prison camp in his novel *One Day in the Life of Ivan Denisovich*. Near the end of the novel, it is Aloyshka the Baptist who conveys to the reader the Christian message on how we are to live. In the last several years, the Baptists have been active in Russia. Many Christian groups of various types from the United States and other countries have poured into Russia to build churches and to spread their message. Groups like the Hare Krishnas and the Aum Shin Rikyo have also won adherents.

Besides Christianity, other religions have traditionally had significant numbers of adherents in Russia. The Russian embassy lists the number of religious associations in Russia as follows: Russian Orthodox, 5,000; Moslem, 3,000; Baptist, 450; Seventh Day Adventists, 120; Evangelicals, 120; Old Believers, over 200; Roman Catholic, 200; Krishnaites, 68; Buddhists, 80; Judaists, 50; Unified Evangelical Lutherans, 39. The embassy estimates the number of believers at 40 percent of the population. Many of the Jews have left in the last decades since they were allowed to emigrate, but the ones still in Russia have been much more active since the fall of communism. Much more numerous are the Muslims, who live mostly in the Caucasus region, near the Volga River, and in Siberia. Many of them are Tatars, whose center is in Kazan on the Volga River. Like other religious groups, the Jews and Muslims suffered in communist times. Both groups have members who are interested in reestablishing ties with others of their religion outside Russia.

Far to the east in Siberia live the Yakut people, also known as the Sakha, whose traditional religion involves shamans, or holy people, healers with supernormal powers. Shamanism was persecuted under the communists, who seized the drums shamans used to induce in themselves a trancelike state, jailed them on trumped-up charges, or declared them insane and kept them sedated in psychiatric hospitals. Shamanism is enjoying a revival among the Yakuts, who have held group seances to cure illness and awaken the spiritual and creative side of people. Highly trained Yakut doctors occasionally incorporate aspects of shamanism in treating their patients.

Other Russians are exploring spiritual avenues outside organized Christian religions. They are once again reading works by adherents of Theosophy, Anthroposophy, and Eastern religions, books by authors such as Madame Blavatsky, Rudolf Steiner, Annie Besant, and George Gurjieff. A whole society is based on the books on yoga philosophy by the early twentieth-century painter Nikolai Rerikh (Roerich) and his wife Elena Shaposhnikova-Rerikh.

Many Russians buy tarot cards, crystals, and incense. Some are convinced that people give off auras reflective of their personalities and temperament, in shades of various colors such as green, red, and blue. Russians are fascinated by UFOs and the paranormal. Even under communism, Russians were much more receptive to accepting paranormal phenomena like auras and extrasensory perception (ESP) than Westerners. Today there are magazines specializing in information about UFOs and psychics and other aspects of the paranormal, like ghosts and visions. Russians also are very fond of astrology, which they use to determine personality and biorhythms and to help make decisions about love and health matters. A team of astrologers was regularly consulted in the 1990s before government decisions were made. Healers, occasionally the descendants of old village sorcerers, and clairvoyants are enormously popular, and some even advertise in newspapers and on television. A television show called *Third Eye* discusses how sorcery can improve one's life. There is a dark side to all these supernatural experiments taking place in Russia. Some evidence of Satanism has arisen, as well as black witchcraft. A well-publicized recent murder occurred in a village because a man was convinced a neighbor woman had used black magic to put a hex on him.

With all of the competition, it is no surprise that the Orthodox Church, given its special history in Russia, pushed for some kind of official protection against its rivals. In 1997, a law was passed recognizing the special historical role of the Orthodox Church in Russia and also recognizing Christianity, Islam, Judaism, and Buddhism as traditional faiths. The law divided religions into two categories, those that could prove that they had been active in Russia for at least fifteen years, which received full legal rights, and those that could not, which would be required to register with the authorities and would face a variety of restrictions. The parliament, the Duma, passed this law over the loud objections of groups like the Hare Krishnas and despite the disapproval of countries like the United States.

Many Russians today consider themselves Orthodox Christians, but do not necessarily practice the religion. The concept of Russia as an Orthodox country is so deeply imbedded that it seems natural to a Russian to be Orthodox. The very word Orthodox means "right belief." To profess Orthodoxy means reconnecting with the past, recapturing aspects of Russian culture that were almost wiped out by the communists.

Russia once was a nation of churches, from the huge ornate gold-domed churches in the Kremlin to the tiny wooden churches in Siberian villages. Today there are still many churches left standing, although most have been stripped bare of their riches and are in need of repair. Once on Russian holidays the air was filled with the sound of church bells ringing, but the communists melted down many of the bells. The communists did carefully maintain many of the famous churches as historical treasures, but undercut their religious function by various methods, such as turning them into museums and banning services.

Orthodox churches often have domes, like the famous onion-shaped domes on St. Basil's in Moscow. The church buildings tend to be square and traditionally do not have seats. Instead, people stand for services. When they pray, they may bend their heads, bow, or kneel, bending forward to touch their foreheads and palms to the floor. The churches are not filled with statues, but have icons, religious paintings. The icons, vividly painted and sometimes covered in precious metals, make the churches very colorful and beautiful. A screen or wall with icons on it, called an iconostasis, divides the church in half. Behind the iconostasis at the eastern end of the church is the area where the sacraments are prepared. Women, who cannot be priests, are not permitted to enter this area. The cross in an Orthodox church has three crossbars instead of one. A small crossbar at the top is for the sign "Jesus of Nazareth, King of the Jews." Near the bottom is a slanted bar, pointing up at one end to indicate the robber who was crucified on the right side of Jesus who accepted him and pointing down on the other to indicate the robber on his left side who denied him. There is no organ in a Russian church. Instead a choir provides the music. The priest chants or sings prayers. Worshipers may move around, placing candles before icons, listening, praying, or crossing themselves. *Gospodi pomilui*, the Russian equivalent of *kyrie eleison* or Lord have mercy is frequently repeated. The main service, similar to the Catholic service but longer, is held on Sunday morning and includes communion as well as singing, Bible reading, prayers, and incense.

The main difference between the Orthodox religion and Catholicism is that the Orthodox do not acknowledge the pope as head of the church. The Russian church does have a hierarchy, and at the head of the Russian Orthodox Church is the Patriarch of Moscow and All Russia. Alexy II, the current Patriarch, assumed his office in 1990. His official seat is presently at St. Daniel Monastery. Other branches of the Orthodox Church in other countries have their own heads. There are two types of clergy, called white clergy and black clergy. The white clergy are married and the black clergy are not.

The Orthodox Church has seven sacraments: baptism, chrismation, eucharist, confession, holy orders, marriage, and anointing the sick. Orthodox Russians are baptized in infancy, usually by immersion, and are chrismated or confirmed right away. Every child is given a saint's name and will celebrate that saint's name day every year. The children are usually given a small cross, which they wear throughout life. Infants also receive communion. In the Orthodox Church, communion consists of both bread and wine, given in a spoon. At weddings, the bride and the groom put on gold or silver crowns to symbolize self-sacrifice and joy and share a cup of wine to symbolize their new, shared life. Divorce and remarriage are permitted. Sex is permissible only inside marriage. Contraception is allowed by the church, but abortion is not.

The Orthodox regard the soul and the body as holy. They revere saints' relics, bones, or even entire bodies. The whole material world is holy, which means that the earth itself is sacred and deserves respect. Each person, who is essentially a representation or icon of God, is precious. Each person has a responsibility not just to think good thoughts, but to actively do good deeds. To Orthodox believers, the Bible is a holy book, but individuals need the

Orthodox Church to help them understand its meaning. Finally, tradition is exceptionally important, the sense that there is a link down through the ages, uniting the community of believers who have done the same things in the same way for hundreds and hundreds of years.

At the end of 1995, a poll of religious beliefs was conducted in Russia by Moscow State University. Of the 3,710 people polled, 37.7 percent declared themselves believers who did not observe religious rituals, and 12.8 percent were observant believers. Of those who declared themselves religious, 71 percent were Orthodox Christians, while another 18 percent were nondenominational. Another study showed a growth in the number of people who believed in God in the early 1990s, but not an increase in the number of Orthodox Christians. The people thought of themselves as just Christians rather than as members of any particular group. In this postatheist society, where those hungry for a spiritual life have many different avenues to explore, the Orthodox Church is not automatically winning back the numbers it lost after the Russian Revolution of 1917. In yet another poll, however, conducted by the Institute for System Studies and Sociology, 44 percent of 1,200 Muscovites polled said they believed in God, and, of those, 65 percent classified themselves as Orthodox. Furthermore, 59.5 percent thought the government should support the church, 69 percent thought there should be religious telecasts on television, half did not object to religious teaching in school, and 82 percent said that destroyed churches should be rebuilt.

Specialists in Russian thought have turned first of all to studying the works of earlier religious thinkers such as Vladimir Solovyov and Nicolas Berdyaev. The study of Marxism-Leninism has been replaced in part by the study of Russian religious thought, in particular to the study of the Russian Idea, the concept developed by Solovyov and others that Russia, with its distinctive culture and religion, has a special mission among the nations of the world. According to this concept, Russia is spiritually superior to other nations, which are materialistic and focus on individualism rather than the collective group. In his book *The Russian Idea*, Berdyaev gives an excellent summation of how many Russians view themselves and how they see their special role on earth. He says that Russians have a certain spirituality, a feeling for the infinite, and a resistance to classifying things in categories. They are given to extremes rather than to moderation. They have a natural wild paganism combined with ascetic Orthodoxy, a tendency toward anarchy, but also despotism. Russians are both cruel and kind, proud and humble. Their special idea is one of living together as a community, of a peaceful life in common, harking back to the Orthodox idea of *sobornost*. It is their divine mission to share this idea with the world.

Other specialists in Russian thought consider themselves adherents of post-modernism, derived from French postmodernism. Mikhail Epstein, a leading theoretician of Russian postmodernism, has noted three tendencies in Russia today and has traced the roots of all three to the immediate prerevolutionary period. The first is the tendency to return to traditional religion, Orthodoxy. The second is neopaganism with its emphasis on the Russian blood, on Russian soil, or on nationalism. The third is minimal religion, religion of no particular denomination which gives a vision of the eventual unification of all religions. Like Berdyaev, he sees Russians as a very spiritual people. He thinks that minimal religion, following upon atheism, allows Russian culture to give a glimpse of a new "post-postmodernist" perspective on spirituality. In other words, once again Russians seem to have the answers.

In addition to thinking of themselves as having deep insight into the human condition (a condition known as "Russian soul") and thinking that they are a special people with a special mission, Russians have a streak of idealism mixed with gloomy fatalism. They are not sure where they are headed, and they worry that the new generation of Russians is more concerned with making ends meet than with late-night discussions about the nature of life. But they are sure that wherever they are going, they will get there in their own special Russian way.

PROVERBS AND SUPERSTITIONS

Russians pepper their everyday speech with proverbs which give clues about their beliefs and their approach to life. There are thousands of these proverbs, with whole dictionaries devoted to them. Some are familiar to English speakers, like "Where there's smoke, there's fire," but many others do not have English equivalents. Russians are very attached to their homeland, and many proverbs reflect this: "At home you don't feel a burden." "At home even the straw is good to eat." "Foreign countries are like a stepmother. They don't stroke the fur in the right direction." They value the group, with friendships running very deep. "Friends won't feel crowded, even in one grave." "Crowded, but not at odds." "Don't have a hundred rubles, but have a hundred friends." Friends rely on one another. "You can't tie a knot with one hand." Lack of generosity is considered a great fault by the Russians. "He has a heart, but it's shut with a little door."

Russians have many proverbs about good and bad fortune. "The rich man even has the wind at his back." "He floats like cheese in butter." "All the pine cones fall on poor Makar." "Angels forge one man's fate with a little silver hammer, for another the devil does it with an ax." Russians believe strongly in fate. "He who is fated to hang won't drown." If things are going well for a Russian, there is sure to be trouble around the corner. "If there's a forest, there's an evil sprite in it." "There was no trouble, so the devil got busy." Death is near, but Russians must not fear it. "Death is not beyond the mountains, but just over your shoulder." "To fear death means not to live in this world." "Be afraid to live, but do not be afraid to die."

Russians have a number of superstitions that help them avoid tempting fate. They do not offer congratulations in advance of a happy event like a birthday lest the fates be tempted to harm the recipient. For the same reason, baby items are not bought in advance of the birth. As among English-speakers, black cats, spilled salt, and broken mirrors spell trouble unless measures are taken to avert the bad luck. As American astronauts learned when working with Russian cosmonauts on the space station Mir, it is bad luck to shake hands across a threshold. Both parties must be either outside or inside. And before taking off on any journey, Russians must sit down quietly for a moment so that the trip will not be a failure.

Some of these sayings and customs are very old. In the modern world, they do not have quite the hold on people that they must have had in earlier times, especially among uneducated people isolated in the country, but the fact that people still use these proverbs and observe these superstitions shows that old ways of thinking still maintain some power in modern Russia.

SUGGESTED READINGS

Berdyaev, Nicolas. *The Russian Idea*. Boston: Beacon Press, 1962.

Edie, James M., James P. Scanlan, Mary-Barbara Zeldin. *Russian Philosophy*. Chicago: Quadrangle, 1965.

Epstein, Mikhail N., Alexander A. Genis, and Slobodanka M. Vladiv-Glover. *Russian Postmodernism*. New York: Berghahn Books, 1993.

Ivanits, Linda J. *Russian Folk Belief*. Armonk, NY: M. E. Sharpe, 1989.

Lossky, Nicholas O. *History of Russian Philosophy*. New York: International Universities Press, 1951.

Rosenthal, Bernice Glatzer. *The Occult in Russian and Soviet Culture*. Ithaca, NY: Cornell University Press, 1997.

Ware, Timothy. *The Orthodox Church*. New York: Penguin Books, 1993.

3

Marriage, Gender, Children, and Education

MARRIAGE BEFORE 1917

A HUNDRED YEARS AGO most Russians were peasants living in the country-side. When it came time for them to marry, and nearly everyone did marry, the young woman customarily moved in with her new husband's family. Because at marriage the boy's family gained a worker, while the girl's family lost one, boy children were preferred over girl children. The boy's parents looked for qualities in a bride that would make her a good worker for their family. They wanted a girl who was big and strong, smart, cooperative, cheerful, industrious, and healthy, one who could work in the fields and weave well and was not promiscuous. A good dowry was an advantage. The girl and boy were usually both in their teens or twenties. The bride might be a few years older than the groom, which was not considered a disadvantage.

Young boys and girls began getting interested in one another in their teens. They might get to know each other very well, because virginity was considered good but not absolutely essential in a bride and the boy's behavior was never an issue. Young love did not always determine whom one would marry because the parents had such a major role in selecting a mate for their son or daughter. But once a mate was decided on, a matchmaker, usually a female relative, was selected to approach the bride's family with an initial offer. The matchmaker was very important, because it was the matchmaker who would present the prospective groom in the best light and try to make the best deal for the family. Sometimes the matchmaker, who was paid for her services, would seek out prospective brides if the boy had not yet found one he liked.

When a choice was made, the matchmaker might speak first with the bride's mother, then the father, and finally the girl herself would be consulted, and the terms of the marriage, that is, what gifts the families would exchange, would be discussed. If that first session went well, the second step was the showing of the bride, a formal occasion when the groom and his family would check out the bride to make sure she did not have any major flaws. These premarital events were accompanied by many special little rituals, meals, gift exchanges, and songs. The bride sang laments, sad at leaving her home to go to a house full of strangers, who would make her work hard and might mistreat her. The night before the wedding, her girlfriends might help her with a ritual bath in the bathhouse to prepare for the ceremony. They might also tell fortunes. While the girls were getting together, the boys might also meet for one last stag party.

On the day of the wedding, the bride dressed in fine clothes. The wedding ceremony was then conducted, during which the single braid she had worn down her back as a girl was combed out, ready to be fashioned into the two braids that married women wore. In the Orthodox service, wedding crowns were raised over the heads of the bride and groom symbolizing the difficult feat they were undertaking by getting married. After the ceremony, the party ate and drank and presented the new couple with bread and salt, symbols of hospitality. Finally the couple went to bed amid much fanfare. Even though the couple was now married, the bride was not yet considered a full member of her new family. That would happen only after she had produced a child.

If a girl was discovered not to be a virgin when the sheets were examined for blood after her wedding night, that was once considered serious business. But as morals loosened by the end of the nineteenth century, fewer and fewer still believed that a married woman should be publicly beaten if she was unfaithful or that an unmarried girl should have the gate to her house smeared with tar. Infanticide and abortion were sometimes still practiced in peasant communities by both married and unmarried women, to conceal a pregnancy, to get rid of an unwanted child, or perhaps for other reasons.

MARRIAGE AFTER 1917

At the time of the Russian revolution in 1917, women were granted equality with men. Some thought that marriage would die out altogether and people would engage in free love, but that did not happen. At the end of the century, marriage was alive and well, although the ceremony had changed quite a bit. Soon after the revolution, the communist government made marriage a civil ceremony rather than a religious one. Instead of going to church, couples went to the registry office, or ZAGS, to get married. Eventually, the ZAGS ceremony took on some fancy trappings, as brides arrived dressed in white gowns and veils and took their vows with their grooms in a "wedding palace" before an official, often with a bust of Lenin overseeing the proceedings in the background. The ceremony consisted of a short statement about the significance of forming a new family, the couple's consent to the marriage, the signing of the register, congratulations, and finally the donning of the rings, which were worn on the right hand. The couple might ride in a car decorated with a bride doll or big wedding rings on the wedding day. The custom arose of going to a war memorial to leave flowers by the eternal flame of the unknown soldier, or alternatively at some other famous site, such as Lenin's tomb. Often the wedding party, consisting of family and friends, would gather for a wedding picture at a well-known site, like the Bronze Horseman in St. Petersburg or the scenic overlook by Moscow University. One feature of the wedding day would be the toast, when the company would shout out *"gorko!"* (bitter!) to indicate that the couple should kiss to sweeten the drinks they were about to consume in their honor.

After the fall of communism, church services for weddings became popular once again. Couples would register officially at the ZAGS and then have a church wedding afterward. Then after touring the sights and taking photos, they would have a lavish feast, often hosted by both sets of parents. Friends and relatives would eat and drink, toast the couple, sing, and perhaps dance. Russian couples have a few days off work for the honeymoon, but often they do not leave town, especially since the party might go on for days.

Today the groom is usually a few years older than the bride, in his early or mid-twenties. Instead of meeting at parties or in the village streets as they once did, young men and women meet at work or at dances or movies or lectures, or just walking on the streets with their friends. The parents and matchmakers no longer have a role in arranging the marriages. Instead the couples form their own attachments, similar to the way such things happen in America. The success rate for marriages is not very high in either country.

LIFE AFTER MARRIAGE

Before the revolution, newlywed peasant couples often moved in with the man's parents. When they had children, three generations would be living under the same roof. The men did much of the field work and cared for horses, while the women took care of the house and the children, did the cooking, and made the clothes. They also worked in the fields and might care for the chickens and cows as well. If they received any wages, sometimes the husband took everything, and sometimes the woman kept her own wages. Typically, some household items were considered hers, rather than his, and she was responsible for some of the household purchases. In the upper classes, women also could own and control property, even land, separate from their husband's, a right they enjoyed much earlier than was the case in the West.

Life at home was hard for peasant women. Not only did they work hard, but they were subject to abuse from their husbands, who frequently beat them if they disobeyed or displeased their husbands in some way. The men were particularly violent when they were drunk on vodka. Of course not all men were abusive, but it must be said that wife beatings were quite common among the peasants in Russia, and sometimes were so severe that the woman died.

One of the goals of the Russian revolution in 1917 was to liberate women from the tyranny of their husbands and from the inferior position they had occupied in society. They were to be considered men's equals and to engage in the building of socialism right alongside them. No longer would they be expected to promise to obey their husbands in the Orthodox Christian marriage ceremony, for marriage was now a secular affair. No longer would peasant women endure rituals like the one in which the father passed a ceremonial lash to the new husband at the wedding ceremony, symbol of his power and authority over her. The regulations of 1917–1918 allowed the Russian woman to choose her occupation and place of residence, and even which surname to use, independent of her husband's will.

As builders of socialism, women would enter into areas of employment formerly occupied by men. This did not affect women in the countryside, the majority of Russians, as much as it did women in the cities. Customs in the countryside changed much more slowly, because there were fewer alternative jobs to farming in the countryside and because both the men and the women resisted change. Women were given control of their earnings and legal equality in the home, but the man was still regarded as the head of the family. Several decades after the revolution, peasant women still did almost all the housework and had many of the menial jobs in the fields, while the men tended to operate any complex farm machinery and occupy any administrative posts.

In the cities, women could and did enter men's occupations, but a woman with a family found herself doing two jobs, her profession as well as the old work of caring for children and the home. Communist planners made some attempts to liberate women from the drudgery of housework and from child care by opening daycare centers and communal kitchens, and by encouraging people to live communally rather than in nuclear families. They also acknowledged the necessity of men's assuming some of women's tasks. But within a decade or so it was clear that the family was surviving and that women would continue to do most of their traditional tasks in addition to having an outside job. There were not enough daycare facilities to meet the demand, nor did all women wish to use daycare. Communal kitchens also did not work out as well as had been hoped. Women still did almost all the cooking and cleaning and child care.

Other attempts to make life easier and more equitable also had their downside. Communist Russia allowed divorce upon request, which resulted in a huge increase in the number of divorces. Some divorces were initiated by women or by couples, but for a certain period, more than half of the divorces were initiated by men, who were involved with other women, quarreling with in-laws, or unhappy that the wife had become pregnant. (Today more women than men file for divorce.) Abortion on demand was also permitted, but in addition to the women who chose abortion, many women were pressured into it by men who did not want a child. In 1936, in an attempt to bolster the family and to discourage the free love rampant in the 1920s, and also to increase the population, the government under Stalin ended the automatic right to abortion, restricting it to situations of dire medical necessity. Divorce was made more difficult, and various forms of support for women were instituted, all in an attempt to stabilize the family and produce more children. Divorce laws and restrictions on abortion were eased once again in the 1950s and 1960s after the death of Stalin.

Although they did not live in a free society, women in late Communist Russia had some advantages that women in 1960s America were still fighting for, such as easy divorce, the right to abortion, entry into trades and professions, access to education, equal rights as the law of the land, maternity leave, and nursing breaks. These and other issues finally came to the fore in America, while Russia could already boast that it had these rights and could also point to many female engineers, judges, and even a cosmonaut. But Russian women did not have the conveniences that made Western women's lives easier. Few women had cars, washers, dishwashers, or even good cleaning agents. They lived in cramped quarters and spent precious time during the lunch break and after work shopping for food and clothing. The clothing was generally of low quality and unappealing. To find food, the women often had to go to several different stores, because one store might carry fruits and vegetables, another dairy products, and so on, and because stores were often out of certain products.

In both Russia and America, one of the trouble spots was the relationship between men and women. Even with equality the law of the land in Russia, attitudes did not change overnight. Although some men helped their wives with housework and child care, many spent most of their nonwork hours with their friends, or watching television, or reading, or just sitting around drinking vodka, spending far fewer hours on shopping, or ironing, or cleaning, or cooking, or taking care of the children than their wives did. Men had more time to improve their work skills, which led to better jobs. They got involved in community work and Communist Party work, which led to their involvement in government. Jobs in heavy industry attracted men, while light industry attracted women. Because heavy industry paid more, men earned more than women. Even in professions that women dominated, like lower level teaching or medicine, the top jobs were held by men. Part of the reason was simple prejudice, because many men and women alike seemed to think that it was better to have men in positions of importance. Although men held almost all the most powerful jobs in the country, much of the heavy, dirty unskilled physical labor at the other end of the spectrum was done by women.

While the women's liberation movement in America was working for many rights that Russian women already had, in Russia there was no parallel mass movement to advance women even further toward equality. Many Russian women wanted more leisure time and better quality goods, rather than to break through the glass ceiling to the top positions of power in their society. Also, in a controlled society where the free exchange of ideas was discouraged, it was hard to drum up support for a mass movement of this sort.

However, in 1979 a small group of women in Leningrad published a journal called *Almanac, Women and Russia*, addressing many of the problems they saw in Russian society. They published it in *samizdat*, that is, they published it themselves using typewriters and carbons since it would hardly get official acceptance by the state publishing house. The secret police, the KGB, reacted immediately, threatening the main editor, Tatyana Mamonova, with arrest if she continued to publish. After the third issue, she was forced into exile. Others involved with the journal were arrested or harassed by the KGB.

The editors of *Almanac* identified numerous issues. They were concerned that women did not have true equality in the workplace and that they carried the double burden of work and child care. Health issues were another major topic. Although Russia did not manufacture the birth control pill, other contraceptive devices were legal, but good ones were often hard to obtain. Women relied on abortion as a method of birth control, and it was not unusual for a woman to undergo multiple abortions, often without adequate painkillers. Women who chose to have a baby might be denied painkillers during labor, and faced a week or more in the hospital, perhaps not even given a shower during that time. Women and issues that concerned women simply did not win the respect and attention of the officials, almost always men, who had the power to change things.

Toward the end of the communist years, the government did become increasingly concerned about the birthrate. Women who worked all day and came home to endless chores were in no mood for large families. In Islamic areas of the Soviet Union the birthrate was high, but in Russia, the typical family had only one child. It was hard enough to bring up a child with a husband who gave only minimal help, and harder still if the marriage broke up, as it often did, and the woman tried to bring up the child alone. Two children made the task infinitely more difficult. It was especially hard when a child became ill, and the woman could not find anyone to stay with her child while she worked. The government began making tentative statements about the joys of staying home with children as a possible solution to the low birthrate. The regime that had with much fanfare liberated women from their traditional role was now suggesting that they might like to try it out again. Some women welcomed this idea, at least in the abstract, while others were uninterested either in giving up their jobs or in becoming dependent on a husband. Yet while they might not wish to give up their jobs, nearly nine out of ten women considered the family their main interest in life, with only 11 percent considering their career their top priority over family.

SOCIETY AND GENDER ROLES AFTER 1991

Despite its shortcomings, the communist regime during its seven decades of rule in Russia paid lip service to the idea of equality between the sexes. Under communism women came to occupy a position in society that was the envy of women in other countries. Some of the gains made by women would be challenged in the final decade of the twentieth century, as the communist regime failed and was replaced by capitalism.

Under communism, advertisements did not constantly bombard women with attempts to sell cosmetics, shampoos, and other products that promised to correct their flaws and lead to success with men. Nor did communists sponsor beauty contests for Miss Legs or Miss Hair. This all changed with the advent of capitalism. Women's worth was destined to be judged much more on their physical appearance than it had been in the past.

The downfall of communism proved devastating for women's employment. Many women were let go from their jobs and replaced by men.

Four out of five of the unemployed in Moscow and St. Petersburg were women. The pay differential between women and men worsened, with employed women no longer making 75 percent of men's salaries as they did in 1991, but only 40 percent just four years later. Older women in particular had a difficult time keeping their jobs or finding new jobs. Some were reduced to peddling goods on the street to stay alive.

Some advertisements for jobs in the 1990s specified men only; those advertisements of lower level jobs open to women carefully described what sort of women were wanted. Secretarial positions often specified what age, like early twenties, and personal attributes, like long legs, the successful candidate should have. Women looking for jobs might enumerate their charms in their own advertisements and state that they were "without complexes," that is, that they were willing to accept invitations of a personal nature from their employers.

Some young women scouting for wealthy husbands became prostitutes for tourists; others placed ads in special magazines or on the Internet to attract a foreign husband so that they could leave Russia. Women's position in the culture was further debased by pornography. During the communist years, Russian society seemed largely free of pornography, possession of which was a crime. Pornography did exist unofficially, much of it homemade. After the fall of communism, pornography became widely available. Rape and all kinds of harassment were very common, and did not receive much official attention. Even the right to abortion came under increasing attack, further undermining women's control over their own destiny.

The issue of homosexuality also came to the fore. No laws prohibited lesbianism, which in any case was not very visible in Russia, but during the communist years lesbians could be put in psychiatric facilities and barred from teaching jobs. Male homosexuality, decriminalized in the early days of communism, was a crime punishable by prison from 1934 to 1993, when sex between consenting adult males was once again legalized. After 1989, small gay and lesbian advocacy groups sprang up. However, most Russians remained quite hostile to the whole idea of homosexuality for males or females.

The tradition of male domination of Russian culture, rooted in peasant culture and bolstered by religion, underlay the lack of regard for women. Even under communism, the attitude that men were better suited to run the country and women were more suited to care for the home and children never really disappeared. Since 1991, the participation of women in government has declined. Political figures and media reporters do not hesitate to characterize women as unsuited for politics, lacking the analytical skills needed for government. Women themselves tend to be rather passive, with few looking to government to solve their problems. They see themselves as more tender, more caring, more self-sacrificing than men, and certainly less masculine and aggressive than American women. They seem very fatalistic about their role as women, and for most of them, feminism or political action of any sort holds little attraction. The group called Women of Russia, an alliance of women's organizations dedicated to nominating women for positions in the Duma, achieved some success in the early 1990s, but it did not have a feminist agenda. There is a small feminist movement in Russia, one of whose members, Anastasiia Posadskaia, attempted unsuccessfully to run for election to the Duma in the 1990s. Whether the feminist movement will ever capture the imagination of Russian women in the future remains to be seen, but for the present it has little power.

EDUCATING CHILDREN

Even under communism, parents believed that boys and girls should be brought up differently and that notion still holds true today. Today parents welcome children of both sexes and think that the ideal arrangement would be to have one of each. Still most parents assume that the lives of boys and girls will proceed along different lines and that the children should be prepared for their separate destinies. Girls should learn to cook and sew and care for the home, and boys should learn to handle rougher chores. Girls should learn to be gentle, charming, and graceful; boys should learn to be brave, strong, and independent. Girls should learn good grooming and spend much more time on their personal appearance than boys. They are considered more delicate, and are admonished not to sit on the cold ground or on cold stones for fear of damaging their ovaries. Boys are thought to be tougher. They must learn how to fight, while fighting is considered unseemly for girls. Boys also learn to extend courtesies to girls, opening doors for them and helping them with their coats.

Women spend much more time with the children than men do. Although the man is usually considered the authority in the house, the woman provides most of the discipline and the affection for the children. The woman may be lucky enough to have the help of the *babushka*, the grandmother, or of her husband, but most of the work falls on her alone. Despite her heavy load, the woman can look forward to a longer life than her husband. Although both sexes live shorter lives now than they did in the later years of communism, women outlive men by more than a decade. Boys are brought up to live on the edge, smoking and drinking and engaging in other risky behavior. Their work brings them into contact with industrial pollutants that shorten life. They also face the prospect of being drafted into the military. Mothers continue to feel responsibility for their children even on the eve of adulthood, and during the Chechen conflicts in the 1990s, more than a thousand Russian mothers came to the front lines to find their sons and take them home, facing down any officials who might object. Some even went into Chechnya, persuading the Chechen captors of their sons that they would never leave until their sons were released to their mothers.

Since the fall of communism, conditions have changed so drastically that it is hard for parents to guide their children as they confront the two big decisions adolescents face, the choice of a profession and the choice of a mate. Russians have been traditionally rather prudish in their reluctance to talk about sex or teach about it in school. The explosion of sex in advertising, on television, and in pornography in the last decade has spawned a sexual revolution in Russia. The rapid rise in sexually transmitted diseases spurred efforts to open centers to disseminate information about family planning and to distribute contraceptives, but not everyone was happy. Opponents claimed that sex education was perverting the youth and causing the birthrate to plummet. Some voiced concern that young people did not properly understand the relationship between sex and love and were engaging in sex too freely and at too young an age.

The choice of a career was also problematic. For girls, the choices seemed fewer. Both girls and boys were in danger of being attracted to high-paying jobs that were dangerous, such as prostitute or hitman or mobster. Many respectable jobs in the old economy simply were not being rewarded with a paycheck at all, and young people were looking elsewhere for work. The new world of business was attractive, particularly for the boys, who did not face the discrimination that girls did. Most of the entrepreneurs in the new economy are male, although there are a number of women who are also starting businesses, some of which have been very successful.

SCHOOLS

The communists set up inexpensive daycare centers to free mothers for outside employment. Even though many mothers preferred to make other arrangements, considering daycare too impersonal or unhealthy for very young children, there were still never enough spaces to take care of all the children who needed daycare. Today daycare is much more expensive and hard to find. Parents of slightly older children are lucky to find care in a facility that teaches them their letters and numbers.

Children begin formal schooling at age six or seven. School traditionally begins on September 1 and ends in late May. Primary school students have a shorter school day than the older children, although some have special arrangements to stay at the school through the afternoon until their parents pick them up after work. The younger children are taught most subjects by a single teacher, who teaches them five or six days a week. Students form close friendships since the homeroom group remains the same throughout their schooling. Their desks, made to be shared by two students, also foster closeness.

Russian children are given a good grounding in academic subjects at a young age, but they are also socialized. In communist times they learned to cooperate in a group setting and put the group ahead of their own personal desires. This training in sharing and self-control began early. Tiny babies were traditionally swaddled, for Russians feared that they might scratch or otherwise harm themselves if left free. The lessons in control continued as children learned that it was bad to monopolize a toy, saying *"moyo!"* (mine!) when they should be sharing. The atmosphere in a Russian classroom was often more orderly than its American counterpart, with, apparently at least, greater respect for authority. As communism began to lose ground, uncertainty arose as to what the moral compass of the new society would be. One attempt to adapt to the new conditions has been the introduction of more attention to individual needs and talents, rather than the subordination of the individual to the group. Another sign of the new individualism has been the abandonment of school uniforms in many educational institutions.

Russian students must attend nine years of school. As they get older, they have different teachers for different subjects. The curriculum is fairly standardized, although some schools may be stronger in one area or another. In school, students study Russian language and literature, history, geography, economics, foreign language, mathematics, physics, chemistry, biology, art, and music. They are graded on a number scale of one to five, with five being the best. Examinations are often oral. Cheating in class is common and is not particularly frowned on. At the end of nine years, students may continue to study academic subjects for two years, go to a vocational school, or get a job. Students on the academic track may take an examination to get into a university or a more specialized institute for five or six more years of education. Higher education in Russia is much more specialized than higher education in the United States. Students are expected to learn one field in depth rather than take a variety of general-education courses as is the practice in America. Many students receive financial support to defray the cost of education. Graduate degrees are much rarer in Russia than in America.

Russian education faces many problems today. School buildings are in poor repair, and some lack heat or even plumbing, particularly in the country. Overcrowded schools must operate in shifts, with some students coming early in the day, and others in the afternoon. The students themselves are frequently in poor health, victims of the environmental problems created by previous generations. Two million Russian children have no families, some living in orphanages and some on the streets. A number of these children never attend school at all. Many teachers have left the profession, discouraged by the low government pay, and those that remain have gone on strike more than once to protest nonpayment of wages and poor conditions.

There have been calls for innovation in teaching methods for two decades, but it is hard to expect those who have been teaching for many years to suddenly change their methods and make learning more student-centered. There was also a call for new textbooks because the old books were out of date. They were filled with communist versions of history, or else they simply did not cover the subjects needed in the new Russia. Teachers in some cases had to continue using the old texts or do without, because economic problems and shortages delayed the production of new materials. Reformers also wanted more flexibility in the curriculum and more input from teachers and parents, although others feared a watering-down of the rigorous educational program. Meanwhile students today are questioning the value of entering the teaching profession, or indeed of pursuing higher education at all. Higher education was once a ticket to a better life, but now the ticket seems to lie in business and in the marketplace.

Some educators are taking note of the new conditions in Russia and the new needs of their students, and not just in the biggest cities. Programs in business management are springing up in various places, and Russia now offers an MBA. Even children are learning about economics. Recently there was a competition for schoolchildren called the Russian Model Economics and Management Olympics, in which the children were divided into teams called "firms" and were asked to manage their firms under changing market conditions. The team from Samara, far from the capital, beat out both St. Petersburg and Moscow.

Although both sexes receive a solid education in Russia, once school is over, the opportunities are at present greater for young men than they are for young women in the new market economy. But women are in a much better position today than they were before 1917, when most of them were illiterate and under the authority of their husbands. Today they have the education and self-confidence to help determine what their position will be in the new society.

SUGGESTED READINGS

Clements, Barbara Evans, Barbara Alpern Engel, and Christine Worobec, eds. *Russia's Women*. Berkeley: University of California Press, 1991.

Creuziger, Clementine G. K. *Childhood in Russia: Representation and Reality*. New York: University Press of America, 1996.

Jones, Anthony, ed. *Education and Society in the New Russia*. Armonk, NY: M. E. Sharpe, 1994.

Lempert, David H. *Daily Life in a Crumbling Empire*. Boulder, CO: East European Monographs, 1996.

Mamonova, Tatyana, ed. *Women and Russia: Feminist Writings from the Soviet Union*. Boston: Beacon Press, 1984.

Marsh, Rosalind, ed. *Women in Russia and Ukraine*. Cambridge: Cambridge University Press, 1996.

Russian Life magazine, especially 3/96, 8/96, 3/98, 5/98, 2–3/99.

Sutherland, Jeanne. *Schooling in the New Russia*. New York: St. Martin's Press, 1999.

Tian-Shanskaia, Olga Semyonova. *Village Life in Late Tsarist Russia*. Bloomington: Indiana University Press, 1993.

Webber, Stephen L. *School, Reform, and Society in the New Russia*. New York: St. Martin's Press, 1999.

Worobec, Christine D. *Peasant Russia: Family and Community in the Post-Emancipation Period*. DeKalb, IL: Northern Illinois University Press, 1995.

4

Holidays and Leisure Activities

HOLIDAYS

FOR MANY CENTURIES Russian holidays were based on a mixture of agricultural observances, many of which were rooted in old pagan customs, and the Orthodox Christian calendar. Much of that changed with the communist revolution of 1917. Many of the old holidays died out or were in some cases converted to secular holidays. New holidays were added. Since the fall of communism in 1991, some of the old traditions are being brought back, while some of the newer holidays are dying out. Although it seems unlikely that all of the old holidays will be resurrected, there is interest in reviving old customs, some of which never completely died out in rural areas.

The year begins with a huge holiday, which resembles both Christmas and New Year's. Before the 1917 revolution, Christmas was celebrated on December 25, but because Russians were still using an old calendar, which lagged thirteen days behind that of the West, the holiday was actually being celebrated on January 7 by modern calculations. (In the twenty-first century, the lag is fourteen days.) For a time under communism, Christmas was officially not celebrated at all. Gradually the customs associated with Christmas became attached to New Year's Day, celebrated January 1. After the fall of communism, Christmas was again observed, still on January 7, since the Orthodox Church had not abandoned the old calendar. Nearly three generations have grown up under communism, however, so the customs associated now with New Year's Day have to a large extent remained there, and Christmas is a more modest celebration. In the 1990s, the largest celebration took place January 1, with some people observing Christmas on January 7, and even some marking December 25, the Western Christmas date, as well as January 14, the start of the new year according to the old calendar.

The holiday season begins in December, as people begin preparations for the New Year. This is the biggest celebration of the year for both adults and children, so the excitement level is high. People shop for presents, which tend to be less numerous and lavish than gifts in America. They also begin planning the holiday meal and laying in supplies for it. People send New Year's cards to each other, often inscribed *S novym godom*, which is the equivalent of Happy New Year. Many people buy a fir tree, called a *yolka*, which resembles a Christmas tree but tends to be skinnier. The word yolka is related to our word Yule. Occasionally there have been shortages of affordable trees, so some people have bought a branch rather than a whole tree. Some people buy an artificial tree, although most do not approve of them. The yolka may be set in a bucket of sand to help keep it moist, and it is decorated with ornaments. The ornaments are of various types, with animals such as wolves, foxes, horses, birds, fish, bears, and squirrels being very popular. There are also balls and little figurines of clowns and snowmen and other characters. Strings of colored lights decorate the trees. Just as the United States has an enormous tree set up in Washington, Russia has one in the Kremlin in Moscow. Huge trees are also set up in public squares, hotel lobbies, and other public places. Children join hands and dance around the fir tree, singing songs about the tree that has come from the forest to be with them for the New Year. Russians first learned about the Christmas tree, a custom imported from Germany, in the time of Peter the Great, but trees were not widely used until the nineteenth century. At one time during Stalin's rule, it was considered dangerous to set up a tree, but the custom was so popular that the tree soon became associated with New Year's rather than Christmas, and returned in all its glory. As New Year's grows closer, children begin to think of the presents they will receive. Russians do not have Santa Claus. Instead, they have Ded Moroz, Grandfather Frost, and Snegurochka, Snow Maiden. Ded Moroz is not quite as fat as Santa, but he does have a long white beard. He often dresses in a fur-trimmed red robe, but the robe may also be other colors, such as blue. He travels in a *troika*, a sleigh pulled by three horses. Snegurochka is beautiful with a long blond braid down her back. She often dresses in a blue outfit trimmed in white fur. Together they may visit children's parties in December, and they will certainly come to bring presents for the children at New Year's. Some Christmas ornaments look like Ded Moroz and Snegurochka, and figures of them are often placed under the tree. There are also toy Snegurochka dolls and Ded Moroz nesting dolls, several wooden dolls one inside the other.

On New Year's Eve, families eat the fanciest meal of the year. They begin with an array of appetizers, then may have soup, a main dish, and dessert. Suckling pig is traditional, but any of a number of other dishes are possible. They drink tea or sometimes coffee, vodka, wine, and champagne, offering numerous toasts. As the evening progresses, people may exchange gifts, sing, dance, and watch a New Year's telecast on TV. At midnight, the famous Kremlin chimes ring out, sounding the New Year. Everyone toasts the New Year. After the children are in bed, the adults continue to party, visiting friends, eating and drinking. It is important to greet the New Year joyously and festively, for Russians believe that the way they ring in the New Year is the way the whole year will turn out. Before the revolution in 1917, people used to dress up in costumes, often as animals like foxes or wolves, and go from house to house, a custom that survives in some rural areas. Even in cities, children still dress up in costume at the New Year's parties held in schools or clubs. Another old custom, fortune-telling, has remained popular. Traditionally, girls consulted tea leaves or cards or wax shapes dropped in water to find out who they would marry or how long they would live, although today other kinds of fortunes are also told. The Orthodox Church frowns on this custom, but many people practice it. Since the fall of communism, the Orthodox Church has sought to remind people of the Christian origins of the holiday, even broadcasting New Year's Eve services on television. After New Year's, people engage in various kinds of winter sports and other entertainment, as many children and adults have a short break at this season. In early January, Orthodox Christians celebrate Christmas quietly, perhaps with a family meal. This used to be the beginning of the Christmas season in Russia, a time of feasting, singing, fortune-telling, and revelry, which ended with Epiphany twelve days later. Some still give a nod to these holidays. Also in January is Students' Day, which was called Tatyana's Day before the revolution. Tatyana was a saint, and on her day in 1755, the University of Moscow was founded. To commemorate that day, students traditionally drank, joked, and played pranks. In 1995, Tatyana's church at the University was reopened, and once again students began to recall Tatyana's Day as they celebrated.

In mid-February, the Orthodox begin to get ready for Lent. Some mark February 23 as an unofficial men's day, parallel to Women's Day on March 8, a day when women and girls are honored with gifts, flowers, cards, and candy. Some husbands take over their wives' chores on that day, preparing a meal, cleaning, and doing the dishes. In February or early March, the Orthodox observe Maslenitsa, eight days of feasting beginning on the eighth day before Lent. Maslenitsa is based on the Russian word *maslo*, which means butter. It is the equivalent of our Mardi Gras, which means Fat Tuesday. This is the time when Russians traditionally ate bliny, or pancakes, which contain butter and are often served with butter. Like many holidays, this one had its origins in pagan times. Before the revolution, it was a time of great merriment, feasting, games, bonfires, and sleigh rides. Following Maslenitsa is the Great Fast, Lent, the longest of the Orthodox fasts. The very devout eat no animal products during the fast. Early in the spring comes April Fools' Day. As people do in America, Russians prepare April Fools' jokes.

Before the revolution, the most important Orthodox Christian holiday was Easter, a holiday surrounded with a great many customs. Orthodox Easter must follow Passover and often falls after Catholic and Protestant Easter. Because after the revolution those who openly practiced religion could face reprisals at work and school, many people avoided openly observing religious holidays. Today Easter is once again being celebrated openly, but not on the scale it once was. The foods most associated with Easter are *paskha*, a kind of cheesecake, and *kulich*, a tall, round, cakelike bread. Eggs, particularly those dyed red, are also essential to Easter. Eggs are often dyed by boiling them with onion skins. People have traditionally taken the kulich, sometimes surrounded with dyed eggs, to church for blessing. The Easter church service begins Easter Eve and is very beautiful. At midnight, people circle the church three times, symbolically looking for Christ's body. Then the priest announces that Christ has risen, *"Khristos voskres,"* and the people respond that truly Christ has risen, *"Voistinu voskres."* After the service, people go home to break the fast, eating and drinking and playing games. The paskha and kulich are served together and are often eaten with an egg dipped in salt. Games include contests, where people pit their egg against someone else's, to see whose is stronger when the eggs' pointed ends are smacked together. In Russia, the Sunday before Easter is called Pussy Willow Sunday instead of Palm Sunday.

May 1 is the international labor day, a day celebrated in many countries. In Soviet Russia, it was a major communist holiday. In recent years, although it has remained a holiday, it was celebrated mainly by those nostalgic for the communist past. In 1999 in St. Petersburg, only 8,000 turned out for demonstrations that once drew many times that number. Some carried a large banner that bore the communist slogan "Workers of the world, unite!" On May 9, Russians remember the end of World War II, a time of terrible suffering that culminated in a great victory over Nazi Germany. Veterans gather to reminisce and recall their comrades. In Moscow, this happens in Gorky Park or in a square near the Bolshoi Theater. On this day, a red flag with a star, similar to the red flag of the communist years when the war was fought, may fly along with the white, red, and blue flag of Russia. Fifty days after Easter is the day of the Holy Trinity, a holiday still observed by some Russians, who decorate birch trees and have a party under them, or decorate themselves and their homes with birch branches, a survival of an old pagan custom.

After the fall of communism in 1991, Russians observed June 12 as Independence Day, the day Boris Yeltsin was first elected president. The holiday was later renamed Russia Day. St. Petersburg celebrates the White Nights in June, the time of year when the sky stays light very late due to the city's extreme northern location. Recently an Arts Festival has been held in the city at that time. July 7 is Ivan Kupalo, an ancient holiday that in Christian times was associated with the feast of John the Baptist. The holiday was once celebrated with lighting bonfires, swimming, and gathering healing herbs, all attempts at purification and warding off evil spirits. A recent celebration in one small Russian city featured a theatrical performance, singing, a bonfire, and a church service.

Before 1991, November 7 was a major holiday commemorating the revolution in 1917 when the communists took over the country. The day continued to be celebrated after 1991, but the big parades and red banners and exhibitions of military might were replaced by much smaller demonstrations by people who still sympathized with communism. The name of the holiday was changed to Day of National Accord and Reconciliation. After the financial crisis of August 1998, the November holiday drew 10,000 demonstrators, a number larger than usual, to the Moscow commemoration. Demonstrators used the occasion to express dissatisfaction with Yeltsin's government, the economy, and with Western influence. To defuse tension, the demonstrators were not allowed to meet in Red Square, where the revolutionary leader Lenin is entombed. Instead they assembled near the old KGB building. Most Russians, whatever their sympathies, did not join the demonstration but observed the day off work by enjoying pastimes with friends or family.

In addition to these holidays, there are several other holidays observed by the Orthodox Church, many with customs surviving from pagan times, but largely forgotten since 1917. A few Russians interested in their past and in folklore have tried to revive some of these customs. There are also several minor secular days, like the new Mother's Day. Then there are days with personal significance, like the birthday and the name day, which commemorates the saint whose name the Russian shares. The custom of marking the saint's day still existed during the communist era to a certain extent, although people tended to celebrate birthdays instead. Today, the custom of celebrating saints' days is becoming popular once again. To celebrate their own special days, people have parties and serve dessert, a pie or cake, and may drink champagne.

Finally, there are jubilees, anniversaries marking significant dates in Russian cultural history. In 1997, for instance, Russians celebrated the 850th anniversary of the founding of Moscow. A concert, laser light show, and many other festivities were planned for the extravaganza, which capped more than a year of construction and cleaning up of the city in preparation for the party. In 1999, Russians marked the 200th anniversary of the birth of their favorite author, Alexander Pushkin, with festivities at places significant to his life. Because of the economic crisis that began the previous summer, the festival was not as large as had been originally planned.

SPORTS, HOBBIES, OTHER ENTERTAINMENT

Russians are very fond of sports and have traditionally done very well in international competitions like the Olympics. Under communism, Olympic sports received state support, and it is not surprising that the condition of sports since 1991 has been affected by the uncertainty of financing that affects every aspect of Russian life. Training facilities have deteriorated with little money to fix them, and several top athletes have left Russia to continue their careers abroad. Nevertheless, conditions are slowly improving, and Russia continues to produce world-class athletes.

One of Russia's favorite sports is ice hockey. The USSR won Olympic gold medals in hockey an amazing six times in the seven games between 1964 and 1988, and took silver the other time. After the Soviet Union split up, Russia still managed to win gold as part of the unified team representing the old Russian republics, and then won silver in 1998. The Russian Hockey League, overseen by the Russian Ice Hockey Federation, has several outstanding teams, but the most famous is Dinamo, whose home stadium is Moscow's Luzhniki Sports Palace. Dinamo, in their familiar blue-and-white, took several titles in the 1990s. Hockey Hall-of-Famer Valery Vasiliev once played for Dinamo, and in recent years outstanding players have included Sergey Petrenko, who played on the 1992 gold-medal team in the Olympics. Other championship teams include Lada from Togliatti, Torpedo from Yaroslavl, Ak-Bars from Kazan, and Metallurg from Magnitogorsk. Interest in ice hockey is strong not just in the capital, but in cities all across Russia.

Another top team sport is soccer. Spartak, the Moscow team dressed in red and white, is currently the best in Russia, winning numerous titles since the fall of communism. Russians avidly follow the careers of such top players as Ilya Tsymbalar and Andrey Tikhonov. Other excellent teams include Lokomotiv, CSKA, and Dinamo, all from Moscow; Rotor from Volgograd; and Alania from Vladikavkaz. Russia has had a difficult time in recent years in international competitions, prompting the government in 1998 to promise more support.

Among individual sports, Russians excel at cross-country skiing and ice skating, naturals for a country that lies so far north. The women skiers are very strong, winning all five gold medals at the Nagano Olympics. Top skiers include Larisa Lazutina, Olga Danilova, and Yulia Chepalova. Russian ice skaters are legendary. Skating as individuals and in pairs, they have consistently won championships. Paired skaters have won ten consecutive gold medals in the Olympics. Russians also excel at ice dancing, in which the pair Pasha Grishuk and Evgeny Platov won gold medals in two Olympics in a row. In 1999, Russians swept the gold medals in all categories of ice skating at the World Championships in Helsinki, the first time a single country had done that.

Tennis has become increasingly popular in the last dozen years. Even government leaders like Boris Yeltsin have taken it up, and fans follow matches eagerly. Among the stars of Russian tennis are the fiery Anna Kournikova and Evgeny Kafelnikov, who play in matches all over the world. Many young people are interested in taking up tennis, although it can be costly to pursue training to be a champion. Until more communities build free courts and cheaper equipment becomes available, tennis will remain a sport for those with some money to spare.

Many ordinary Russians enjoy not just watching, but playing, sports. Besides the sports mentioned earlier, Russians engage in a variety of sports, including, for instance, basketball, volleyball, bowling, karate, cycling, gymnastics, rock climbing, mountain climbing, caving, auto racing, sailing, alpine skiing, sky diving, ballooning, swimming, diving, archery, boxing, wrestling, squash, hunting, fishing, baseball, fencing, inline skating, roller blading, bodybuilding, golf, horse racing, billiards, table tennis, and even paintball. One other activity very widely practiced is walking in the woods collecting mushrooms, if that might be considered a sport. Obviously, some of these sports are limited to those with the money to pursue them, but still there is a fairly wide range of activities available.

People pursue quieter hobbies as well. Many people are collectors. They build and collect model boats and cars; they collect coins and stamps and insects. A new hobby is collecting phone cards in various denominations from different cities. People keep dogs and cats, garden, and take photographs. They sew and knit and work crossword puzzles and play games like backgammon and checkers and cards. One very popular card game is called Fools. There are clubs for every conceivable interest, including a bonsai club and a radio club. People are increasingly interested in computers and like to design web pages and share their interests with others on the Internet.

One quiet activity that Russians are famous for is chess. There are chess clubs everywhere in Russia, with names like "Chemist" and "Siberia" and "Kings." Seven-member teams compete in contests like the Russia Championship and the Chess Festival Open. Of the top twenty players listed by the World Chess Council in 1999, eight were Russian, including three of the top five. Few women have yet reached the top ranks in world chess, and the Russians are no exception. The teams tend to be all-male, and all eight Russians on the list of top twenty players are male. There is, however, a separate Russian Women's Championship, which was won in 1999 by Yulia Demina.

Russians have made an excellent showing for decades in chess. Only rarely has the world champion been from some country other than Russia. Alexander Alekhine, Mikhail Botvinnik, and Boris Spassky are only a few of the well-known champions from earlier in the century. In 1985, champion Anatoly Karpov was defeated by Garry Kasparov, who has dominated chess to the present day. Kasparov was a grandmaster while still a teenager and became the youngest world champion ever when he defeated Karpov at the age of twenty-two. At twenty-six, he received the highest rating ever recorded for a chess player. Today he is regarded by most as the finest player who ever lived. In 1989, he beat a computer at chess, and did it again in 1996. When he lost to IBM's Deep Blue in a 1997 match, the news flashed around the world. Six million fans reportedly followed the six-game match on the Internet.

In the 1990s Russians discovered video games. Computer use is by no means as widespread yet in Russia as it is in America, but it is growing rapidly. Many Russian organizations and individuals have Websites, and using computers for entertainment is increasing as more people get access to computers. There are also more than one million PlayStation systems in Russia, both PAL systems and modified American and Japanese systems. Nintendo has not yet arrived in any significant numbers. Russians play foreign games like Sim City 3000, but also domestically produced games. In 1994, there were only three or four game developers, but soon there were ten times that number. The most famous Russian game so far has been *Tetris*, although *Rage of*

Mages has also done well. At the end of the twentieth century, Russians were completing work on much-anticipated new games, such as one known in the planning stages as *Allods 3D*, a 3-D role-playing strategy game by the *Rage of Mages* developers. Other new games in development were *Iron Strategy* and *Warlock Vseslav: Sword of Fire*. Russians bring a great deal of technical expertise, beautiful intricately detailed artistry, and storytelling ability to their work in this field, just as they do to their more traditional expressions of culture such as crafts.

Russians have many other ways of enjoying themselves. They entertain friends, go to restaurants, stroll in the parks, go to zoos, dance, listen to music, and engage in dozens of other activities. One form of entertainment that has achieved worldwide fame is the circus. The government-sponsored Russian State Circus Company includes forty-two permanent circuses, as well as traveling circuses. The Russian circus has long been known for its artistry and outstanding performances. Some cities like Moscow have permanent facilities for circuses. The Moscow Circus, long considered one of the finest in the world, has more than one thousand people involved in its productions and has won many prizes. The Moscow Circus clowns, especially Oleg Popov and Leonid Kostyuk, are widely known in Russia. Other contemporary acts include Natalya and Alexey Panarin's performance, in which they cause birds to appear and disappear and turn into other birds. As has happened in almost every other area of Russian life in the past decade, the Russian circus has fallen on hard times, with financial support sometimes lacking for salaries, training, and essential repairs.

SUGGESTED READINGS

Christmas in Russia. Lincolnwood, IL: Passport Books, 1993.

Gerhart, Genevra. *The Russian's World: Life and Language*. New York: Holt, Rinehart, and Winston, 1994.

Russian Life magazine, especially 1/93, 1/96, 12/97–1/98, 1–2/00 for holidays; most issues for sports.

The Internet is also a good source for sports information.

5

Cuisine and Fashion

CLASSIC CUISINE

RUSSIAN CUISINE reached its peak of excellence in the century before the 1917 revolution. It was based on the simple food of early Russia, the content of which was determined naturally by the northern climate. The short summers encouraged the storage of fruits and vegetables through pickling and preserving to last through the long cold winters. Cabbages, mushrooms, and berries of all sorts, preserved by women in the short growing season, made their way into pies and soups, staples of early cuisine, throughout the year. Cabbage, made into a kind of sauerkraut, provided much of the vitamin C for the population. Preserved in a method introduced by the Tartars during their long occupation of Russia, sauerkraut was in turn used to make *shchi*, cabbage soup, one of the staples of peasant cuisine, along with bread and buckwheat groats, or *kasha*. Russians have a saying, *"Shchi da kasha, pishcha nasha,"* which means shchi and kasha are our food. Mushrooms and berries were plentiful, and Russians were familiar with not only a large variety of berry types, but also many different types of mushrooms.

Religion also played a role in determining cuisine, since the Orthodox religion imposed fasting on more than half the days each year. Russians were to fast for seven weeks before Easter, forty days before Christmas, for periods before the feast of the Assumption of the Virgin in August and the Feast of Peter and Paul in June, as well as most Wednesdays and Fridays. Fasting meant that people were to give up animal products such as meat, eggs, and dairy products. This meant that Russians would develop many meatless dishes, relying instead on fruits, vegetables, grains, and fish.

Over the centuries, contact with other lands introduced buckwheat, rice, tea, spices, noodles, and many other foods, including potatoes, which became a staple of Russian cooking, as they did in so many other countries. Russian territorial expansion introduced foods from conquered areas, in particular the foods of Central Asia and the Caucasus, rice and lamb dishes and kebabs. After Peter the Great opened up Russia to the West, Russian rulers and aristocrats began bringing in chefs from Europe, who brought with them the great cuisines of their native lands, especially that of France. All these influences together created classic Russian cuisine, which was well known in the nineteenth century, but was in danger of being forgotten after the long years of communist rule came close to destroying the traditions.

Although Russian cuisine benefited from foreign influence, it also gave some gifts to other cuisines. Most people would immediately associate caviar and vodka with Russia, and some would think of borscht, a soup colored red by beets, and beef Stroganov. The dessert baba au rhum is based on the Russian baba, a kind of cake or sweet bread, with the addition of rum. *Baba* is the word for woman or peasant woman. One dish that sounds as if it should be Russian is the delectable dessert charlotte russe, which is French for Russian Charlotte. It was created by Antoine Carême, French chef to the tsar, but is unknown in Russia today. Veal Orlov is another dish created by the French, and named for a prominent Russian, that is unknown in Russia. Russian dressing—mayonnaise and ketchup with some other flavorings—is an American invention with no Russian roots.

The biggest Russian contribution to other cuisines is not a dish, but the method of serving meals. When the French chefs came to Russia, they noticed that meals were not served in the fashion then popular in France at fancy dinners. When people sat down at a meal in France, the table was already laden with many dishes, with several different varieties of hors d'oeuvres, soup, and fish, all losing quality as they awaited the guests. Later, the main dishes would be set on the table, and, finally, the desserts. In Russia, the dishes, far fewer in number than the several dozen served in France, were served one at a time, which meant they had a much greater chance of being eaten while at the peak of perfection. Although there was some resistance from chefs who loved the elaborate constructions of food displays in the French fashion, most came to realize the culinary benefits of the Russian service, and by the late nineteenth century, the Russian method was adopted by prominent chefs in France, and therefore in the rest of the West. Today in restaurants when we are served first the appetizer, then the soup, the main dish, and dessert, each in its own turn, we are following the Russian custom of long ago.

It is difficult today in Russia to imagine the glory of Russian cuisine enjoyed by the middle and upper classes in the nineteenth century. The great literature of the nineteenth century is filled with references to food, and from their reading Russians can get an idea of what has been lost nearly beyond recall. The food in the literary descriptions is of immense variety, very rich, and served in great quantities, almost unimaginable in Russia of the communist and post communist years.

The author most associated with the enjoyment of food is Nikolai Gogol, whose descriptions of food are legendary. When Korobochka hurries off to have a small bite prepared for her unexpected guest Chichikov in *Dead Souls*, Chichikov soon finds himself looking at a table loaded with "small mushrooms, patties, hasty puddings, scones, tarts, pancakes, and wafers with all sorts of baked additions—baked chopped onion, baked poppyseed, baked curds, baked clotted cream—and Heaven alone knows how many other things were there. 'This is an unleavened turnover with eggs!' the hostess informed him" (60).

The best single description of a Russian meal, however, has to be the one in the short story "Siren" by Anton Chekhov. In the story a court secretary describes a meal in such loving detail, course by course, that the justices he is working with run out one by one, unable to resist the thought of eating. He begins his meal with vodka,

And you don't just gulp it down, straight off, but first you sigh, you rub your hands together, you gaze nonchalantly at the ceiling, and only then, slowly, you raise it to your lips, and at once sparks from your stomach flash through your whole body. . . . The best appetizer is herring. You eat a bit of herring with onion and mustard sauce, and without waiting, my friend, while the sparks are still flying in the stomach, you help yourself to caviar, with lemon juice, if you prefer it that way, then you have a radish with salt, and another piece of herring. (92)

Eventually he gets around to the meat pies and soup course,

The meat pie must make your mouth water, it must lie there before you, naked, shameless, a temptation! You wink at it, you cut off a sizable slice, and you let your fingers just play over it, this way, out of excess of feeling. You eat, the butter drips from it like tears, and the filling is fat, juicy, rich, with eggs, giblets, onions. (93)

He goes on to describe the soups, the fish, and eventually the roast.

> If you take a duckling, one that has had a taste of ice during the first
> frost, and roast it, and be sure to put the potatoes, cut small, of course,
> in the dripping-pan too, so that they get browned to a turn and soaked
> with duck-fat. (95)

The dinner ends with spiced brandy, a smoke, and then off to bed with the newspaper.

Upper-class Russians also enjoyed fancy restaurant meals, like the famous meal at the Anglia (England) restaurant in Moscow in *Anna Karenina*, where Stiva dines on oysters, followed by clear soup with vegetables, turbot with thick sauce, roast beef, capons, and fruit salad, or as the waiter thinks of it, "Soupe printanière, turbot sauce Beaumarchais, poulard a l'estragon, macédoine de fruits," accompanied by various wines and ending with cheese (Tolstoy, 48). His friend joins him in this meal, although he protests that he would rather have shchi and kasha, the simple cabbage soup and buckwheat groats that a peasant might eat for his dinner.

THE MAIN MEAL AND INDIVIDUAL DISHES

The traditional Russian main meal begins with appetizers, called *zakuski*. The zakuski course is a real marvel, one of the finest creations in the history of Russian cuisine. Usually more than one appetizer is served, and for a special meal there might be more than a dozen or even two dozen. It is uncertain how the custom of serving zakuski arose, but it may have come about as a way of feeding guests who traveled long distances in the country and whose arrival times could not be predicted with much accuracy. They could be fed with small snacks while a meal was being prepared for them. Whatever the origin, the custom was well established before the nineteenth century. Zakuski are usually served to guests seated around a table, although a buffet arrangement is also possible.

No meal at any time of day is complete without bread, which together with salt is the traditional symbol of Russian hospitality. At the main meal, it appears on the table immediately, with the zakuski course, piled up in thick slices. Russian bread is delicious and is more substantial than most American bread. There is white bread, black bread, which is mostly rye, and gray bread, a mix of rye and wheat. Butter is usually served alongside the bread.

The most famous dish served as part of the zakuski course is caviar. Caviar is fish roe, or fish eggs, preferably preserved whole and *malossol*, which means lightly salted. Although the roe of many types of fish can be eaten as caviar, the best comes from sturgeon. Of sturgeon caviar, the rare sterlet variety, golden in color, was once considered the finest, but it has virtually disappeared today. Beluga roe, the largest sturgeon roe, is now considered the best. Ossetra and sevruga are other good sturgeon roes. All are varying shades of grayish-black in color. The Caspian Sea, the source for much of the sturgeon caviar, is at risk from overfishing and pollution, and today good caviar is quite expensive. Russians are also fond of salmon caviar, which is reddish. The eggs are large and tasty, and much less expensive than sturgeon roe. Caviar should be served in a glass container, and may be eaten plain, or on thin white bread, sometimes lightly toasted, sometimes buttered. Some sprinkle lemon on caviar, while others prefer it with chives, and still others want nothing to distract from the pure taste of the caviar itself.

Fish also regularly appear in the zakuski course. Pickled herring served with a mustard or sour cream sauce or with an oil and vinegar dressing is very common. Eel, sardines, salmon, sturgeon, and other fish may also be served. The preparation may be as easy as opening a can, or may be as elaborate as encasing a whole fish in an aspic surrounded by garnishes or caviar, cucumbers, or crayfish tails. Sliced meat, marinated mushrooms, radishes, pickles, and sauerkraut are old standbys on the zakuski table. Sometimes vegetables are marinated or mixed with oil and vinegar or mayonnaise to make a kind of salad, like beet salad or cucumber salad. A very common summer salad is cucumbers and tomatoes in sour cream. Another common salad is a vegetable vinaigrette colored red by beets. Salad Olivier, invented by a French chef at his Moscow restaurant the Ermitazh (Hermitage) in the 1860s, once contained crayfish, truffles, and grouse, but today is made simply of chicken, pickles, hard-boiled eggs, peas, and onions, mixed with mayonnaise, and sometimes mounded in a pyramid shape and garnished with hard-boiled eggs and olives. Many other dishes, hot and cold, can be served on the zakuski table, including little meat pies and stuffed vegetables. It is no wonder that a person, filling up on the many delicious treats available, and washing it all down with little glasses of vodka, might think that dinner was over after a single course.

The main meal of the day will have soup after the zakuski. Russian peasants in the past existed largely on soup, usually shchi, but also borscht and ukha. The very poor might have few vegetables in the soup other than cabbage, making it shchi, or if it also had beets it was then considered borscht. Borscht, actually Ukrainian in origin, in a more developed version has cabbage, beets, onion, carrots, potatoes, tomatoes, meat, and other ingredients and is served

Conard High School Library

West Hartford, Conn.

with a dollop of sour cream on top. A third basic soup is *ukha*, or fish soup, which can be made with a single kind of fish or a mixture. It is served clear, with perhaps a piece of fish floating in it. Other traditional soups are barley and mushroom soup and *rassolnik*, made of kidneys and pickles. Savory pies of various sorts may be served with the soups. *Pirozhki* are tiny pies or tarts, so popular they have been sold by street vendors. *Kulebiaka*, known in the West as coulebiac, is a larger pie often filled with a salmon mixture and served in slices.

The main course will probably feature meat with garnishes of some sort. The dish most closely associated with Siberia is *pelmeni*, meat-filled dumplings. In Siberia, pelmeni are traditionally filled with horse meat and are served with vinegar. In western Russia they are filled with beef and are often served with butter instead of vinegar. Despite the fact that under communism the religious fasts were no longer kept by most people, fish remained an important main dish. Pollution and overfishing have reduced the number and variety of fish in Russia, so that many dishes that were eaten in the nineteenth century have disappeared. The greatest of all fish was considered to be the sturgeon, which in modern times has been very hard to find for sale in Russia. Fish might be poached, baked, or sauteed and served in a sauce of some sort. Traditionally, meats and fowl were cooked whole or in very large pieces, and the fashion of cooking smaller pieces was for a long time considered a European novelty. Some of the most famous dishes, like chicken Kiev and beef Stroganov, were developed in the new style. Beef Stroganov has been reduced to cream of mushroom soup and hamburger on noodles by some American cooks, but properly it should be made with the very best cuts of beef, sour cream, mushrooms, and onion, and served with thick fried potato sticks. Chicken Kiev, or *kotlety po-kievski*, originally a Ukrainian import, features fried breaded chicken breasts, pounded thin and stuffed with butter that should come spurting out when the chicken is pierced by a fork. Chicken Pozharsky, *kotlety pozharskie*, is named for its creator, who originally used wild partridges or grouse to make his ground-meat coquettes fried in butter and garnished with mushrooms. Of course, there are many other types of dishes, casseroles and sausages and stews of all sorts. Even *kasha*, cooked buckwheat, might be a main dish, served with butter or milk, or mushrooms and onions. Potatoes are a favorite side dish. At home, Russians are particularly fond of potatoes baked or boiled in their skins, but more complex preparations are served on special occasions and in restaurants. One popular preparation is potatoes with mushrooms and sour cream and onion.

For dessert, ice cream might be served. Russian ice cream is very rich and absolutely delicious. Most ice cream traditionally is vanilla and is often served with jam. There are also various types of cakes and a few kinds of cookies, as well as European-style pastries, some of which have strayed rather far from the original. The very popular napoleon, for instance, in its Russian variant has alternate layers of custard cream and short pastry and looks and tastes different from the West European napoleon. Two old traditional Russian desserts are *kompot* and *kisel*. Kompot, fruit compote, is often served in a glass; kisel is a fruit puree mixed with sugar and potato starch.

HOLIDAY MEALS

Some Russian holidays are associated with special foods. Before the advent of communism, to mark the end of winter Russians celebrated Maslenitsa, Butter Week, a period of revelry before the great fast leading up to Easter. Now that communism is gone, some are reviving these old customs. The food customs during this period have their roots in pagan times, when people celebrated the return of the birds, as well as the return of the sun that would warm the seed and make their crops sprout. About ten days before the beginning of Maslenitsa, Russians baked and ate rolls shaped like larks, with raisins for eyes. Then during Maslenitsa, they made *bliny*, pancakes round and golden like the sun. Bliny are a little thinner than pancakes, and about six inches across. They are eaten with butter and sour cream. Other possible toppings are caviar, salmon, herring, sturgeon, and jam. Bliny were made at home, in restaurants, and by street vendors during Maslenitsa. People might eat a dozen, or even several dozen, at one time, washed down with vodka, plain or flavored.

After Maslenitsa came the Great Fast, Lent, when no animal products except possibly fish were to be consumed. The fast ended at Easter, which also featured special foods. Just before Easter, women made the two traditional dishes, *kulich* and *paskha*. Kulich is a tall cylindrical cake made of flour, milk, sugar, eggs, yeast, salt, with saffron or other flavorings and candied fruit or raisins added. After it is baked, the top may be covered with white frosting or marked with XB, the Russian abbreviation for Christ Has Risen. The kulich is often surrounded by dyed Easter eggs on a small plate and topped with a tall thin candle and perhaps a paper flower, ready now to be blessed at the church during the midnight Easter service before it is eaten. The priest sprinkles holy water on the array of kuliches, their candles flickering in the dim light. Paskha is a kind of cheesecake, made of cottage cheese, eggs, and cream, dotted with raisins, almonds, and candied fruit. It is usually placed in a special mold, which produces a paskha in the shape of a pyramid with XB and a cross on the sides. The kulich will be sliced, and served with a bit of the paskha on the side.

Before leaving for church on Saturday night, all the food is ready for the feast that will begin when the churchgoers return in the middle of the night. The feast, in addition to the paskha and kulich and of course vodka, might include ham, turkey, and a whole suckling pig, platters of cold game, salads, desserts, and many other dishes, for this is the biggest religious holiday of the year. Many people have a lamb made of butter on the table and decorate the table with flowers or greenery. The feast lasts for days, as friends and relatives begin visiting each other on Easter, eating and drinking and playing games.

The ancient ritual food *kutia* is served on Christmas Eve with almond milk. Originally made of wheatberries, honey, and poppy seeds, today it might also be made with rice, raisins, and almonds. It is served in a bowl set in hay to symbolize the Nativity. The other foods served that night must contain no animal products, because the fast before Christmas has not yet ended. Kutia was once also served at funerals. Both Christmas and New Year's may be greeted with some special dish like chicken or goose, although there is no set food that must be served.

The nameday, the day devoted to the saint for whom a Russian is named, was once celebrated even more than the actual birthday, and is once again receiving attention in Russia. The person celebrating the nameday invited family and friends to a party, where *krendel*, a sweet bread in the shape of a pretzel, was traditionally served. Today it is the custom for the person having a birthday to invite friends to a nice meal. The friends bring presents and deliver toasts to the birthday person during the meal. There is a birthday cake with candles.

In Russia, women do most of the home cooking, but on March 8, Women's Day, some men try their hand at cooking a special meal for their wives. There is no particular menu connected with this day.

BEVERAGES

The most famous of all Russian beverages is vodka. The secret of distilling was probably introduced to Russia by merchants from Genoa around 1400 and vodka was definitely made there by the late 1400s. Before vodka, Russians drank mead, which was made from honey. Vodka could be made from various types of grain or other plant matter, and the best, it was found, was that filtered through charcoal made from the Russians' favorite tree, the birch.

The word vodka may come from the word *voda*, meaning water, or it may be derived from the Latin *aqua vitae*, water of life. Russians have been drinking vodka in great quantities for hundreds of years. For much of that time, production was under the control of the state, and produced a lot of revenue. Sometimes the state has tried to encourage temperance by limiting production, but with little effect. The tsarist regime and later Lenin tried to halt drinking just a few years earlier than prohibition was tried in the United States, but by the mid 1920s the effort was abandoned. When Gorbachev attempted to limit drinking in the 1980s, the result was a sugar shortage as people decided to make their own, for which sugar was necessary. Moonshine is known as *samogon* in Russian.

Vodka in its pure state is clear and is drunk straight, not mixed in cocktails or thinned with water or even served on the rocks. It may be drunk from a little glass called a *riumka*, and it is not supposed to be sipped. Once a bottle is opened, the group is expected to finish it. When toasts are given, smart drinkers follow the shot with a drink of water and some food, perhaps a piece of sausage, to counteract the effects of the vodka. Men are expected to drink in quantity, but women do not have to keep up with the group.

Vodka is usually 80 proof, which is 40 percent alcohol. In addition to the plain variety, vodka may be flavored. There have been more than a hundred different types of flavoring over the years. Some flavors are orange, strawberry, cinnamon, coffee, lemon, bison grass, and pepper. Plain vodka is the most common.

Other common alcoholic drinks are cognac; wine, which tends to be rather sweet; and beer. Beer has become increasingly popular in recent years, after years of decline. Because excessive vodka drinking has caused such severe health problems in men, beer drinking is considered a good thing, since beer has so much less alcohol content than vodka. *Kvas*, a drink with one percent alcohol, is so popular that it is sold on the streets in the summer. Kvas is made of rye bread, water, yeast, and sugar and is lightly fermented into a brownish, pleasant-tasting drink. In addition to serving as a drink, it is used as a base for soup.

Of nonalcoholic drinks, Russians tend to avoid tap water in favor of bottled mineral water or carbonated water, which may be flavored. They also sometimes drink bottled juice. Milk and coffee are consumed rather less than in America. What Russians do drink a lot of is tea, hot and sugary. They do not drink iced tea. Tea is usual at breakfast and is also served after the midday and evening meals. Tea traditionally was prepared in a *samovar*, although today it may be made using boiling water and a simple little teapot. In the old days before electricity, a samovar was a regular part of Russian house furnishings, introduced by the Mongols during their long occupation of Russia hundreds of years ago. A samovar was an urn full of water with a spigot. A pipe down the center of the urn was filled with burning charcoal, which heated the water in the urn. An extension fitted on the pipe vented it through the stove's chimney and was removed when the samovar was taken to the table. In warm weather the samovar could be heated up outside. When the water was piping hot, a teapot filled with very strong tea was set atop the samovar. A bit of strong tea was poured for each individual and then diluted with water from the samovar. Tea could be drunk from cups or from glasses set in fancy metal holders with handles. Traditionally, women more often drank from cups, and men from glasses. Russians might add sugar or jam to the tea, or clutch sugar between their teeth and suck tea through the sugar. The old samovars were often made in Tula and were quite beautiful, gleaming brass with wooden handles, or sometimes silver. Today there are electric samovars, utilitarian silver in color and easier to use, but without the soft shine of the older ones.

MEALS

Russians usually eat three meals a day. The first meal is breakfast. People have tea and bread, and some other form of food, like egg, cheese, potatoes, meat, kasha, or leftovers from yesterday's meals. One favorite is *kefir*, a milk product similar to thin yogurt, served in a glass and often sweetened with the addition of sugar. Breakfast tends to be rather substantial. The main meal of the day might be in the middle of the day, when breads, an appetizer, soup, main dish, and dessert are served. If a big meal has been eaten at lunchtime, then dinner in the evening tends to be lighter, with appetizer, main dish, and dessert. Between meals there might be snacks, especially chocolate, of which Russians are exceptionally fond. Tasty Russian chocolate bars come in very colorful wrappers with bright pictures on them. Russians also like other kinds of candy, sunflower seeds, and eskimo pies filled with delicious ice cream.

In the new economy, some Russians are tending to eat more lightly midday and have the larger meal at night. Some skip the midday meal entirely if they cannot afford it. In the late 1990s, Russians were eating much less fruit and meat and fish and fewer vegetables than ten years earlier because of the economic situation.

SHORTAGES

Under communism, Russian cuisine suffered a great deal. When women entered the workforce in large numbers, they had much less time to cook. The communist emphasis was on heavy industry rather than on consumer products, and with the problems in agriculture and transportation, the supply of many types of food declined in quality, quantity, and variety, so even if women had the time to cook, they could not prepare many of the dishes from the cookbooks of the previous century. The feasts of Gogol, Tolstoy, and Chekhov were just a memory.

In communist times, shopping for food could be difficult. Russians lagged far behind the West in developing both frozen foods and convenience foods. There were always shortages of one kind of food or another, and people learned to carry around a mesh bag called an *avoska*, which means perhaps, in case they happened to pass a store where some choice item was on sale. Today a wide range of foods, foreign and domestic, is available in the cities, but many of the items carry a price that most Russians cannot afford. In the country, the items might not even be available at all. Frustrated at high prices and the unavailability of some foods, some Russians try to supplement by growing a bit of their own food, at the weekend *dacha*, (country house) if they live in the city.

Considering only the ordinary essential foodstuffs, Russia at present cannot produce enough food to feed its people and so must depend on imports. But those imports, if they happen to be subsidized or even smuggled in to avoid customs, create an uneven field for domestic competitors trying to produce native Russian products of a quality and at a price that will attract the customer. Reforms in agriculture, transportation, production, marketing, and government policy will, with luck, eventually put Russia in a position to be more self-sufficient.

DINING OUT

Russians love their own cuisine, with its sour and dill flavorings, rich but not spicy. But they have also added to their repertoire by embracing foods from many areas of the former Soviet Union, including rice and lamb pilaf from Uzbekistan and *shashlyk* (shishkebab) from Georgia. In communist times, two of the favorite restaurants in Moscow were the Uzbekistan, which served Uzbek food, and the Aragvi, which served Georgian food. If one was fortunate enough to get in a nice restaurant, the whole evening could be spent talking to friends, drinking, eating, and dancing. Dining out in this fashion was, and is, reserved for special occasions.

Besides the state-run restaurants, in the final years of communism, cooperative-venture restaurants began to spring up; they were expensive, but served fine food, such as Indian cuisine. In the 1990s, many exotic choices sprang up for rich Russians, especially in Moscow. There were restaurants specializing in Russian food, but also restaurants serving Italian, Dutch, Japanese, Tex-Mex, Mexican, French, Scandinavian, American, Polynesian, German, Canadian, and Philippine food. Mexican food seemed especially popular. At the Muskhed (Moosehead), Russian, European, and Canadian food were served, along with ten kinds of beer. The Angara had pigs' feet and a sushi bar. At the Tex-Mex Armadillo, one could eat and then play pool. The Angleter offered an eclectic menu and a 1920s atmosphere. The Mario offered Italian food, while the Luxor offered European, Russian, and Japanese food, along with a light show and DJs. The Posolsky (Ambassadors) Club had French cognac, single-malt whisky and cigars, while the restaurant at the Metropole Hotel, bearing the name of the great Russian singer Chaliapin, offered "koktail" and "longdrink."

Expensive restaurants offering Russian food listed as specialties dishes reminiscent of the luxurious tsarist days. The Sudar (Sir) featured sturgeon boyarstyle, boyars being Russian aristocrats, and steak *dvoryanin*, a dvoryanin being a nobleman. Another restaurant had salmon Tsar Nikolai, as well as dishes named for old noble families. Yet another (the Robin Gud, or Robin Hood) offered both European and Russian food, with the specialty being eels tsarstyle. The Restaurant 1, Red Square, located at the Historical Museum, specialized in extravagant dinners devoted to a special event, such as the Literary Dinner in Honor of Nikolai Gogol, or the Utopian Dinner in the Style of the Russian Avant Garde of the 1920s and 1930s, or a special Easter dinner.

Slightly cheaper were the fast-food restaurants that invaded Russia, on the heels of the earlier invasion by Pepsi and then Coca-Cola. Russians eagerly awaited the opening of the first McDonald's in Moscow. Its spotless restaurant, "Big Mak," and smiling servers all made an excellent impression. The food was expensive by Russian standards, but not as expensive as the pizza at Pizza Hut which soon followed. A Venezuelan of Russian descent opened Patio-Pizza, capitalizing on the new taste of Russians for pizza. Baskin-Robbins opened, and even though it had such a large variety of flavors, the wonderful Russian ice cream held its own.

A Russian version of a fast-food establishment, Russkoe Bistro, opened in the mid 1990s. Russkoe Bistro served Russian pies, kvas, and miniature bottles of vodka, familiar fare and welcome to those who wanted Russia to stop aping the West and go its own way, whatever that might turn out to be.

TRADITIONAL COSTUME

For most of their history, the vast majority of Russians were peasants who wore clothing made in their villages, out of cloth they wove themselves, although supplemented more and more as time went on by material made commercially. Clothing varied by area and also by the economic status of the peasant. Some were rather well off and could afford to own holiday clothing made of fabrics like silk and decorated with gold and silver thread or jewels. Most dressed more simply. Common fabrics were linen and wool. Cotton was also used. If clothes were dyed, red and blue were the preferred colors. The men wore long loose shirts which opened off-center rather than straight down the middle, belted over pants. Instead of socks, they wound cloth strips around their legs. They wore tall felt hats in summer and fur hats when it was cold. They had light coats called caftans as well as heavier ones lined with fur for winter. Footwear consisted of shoes made of strips cut from the linden tree and woven together. In colder weather they wore felt or leather boots.

The women wore a long-sleeved garment. Married women in the north might cover this with a kind of jumper or pinafore called a *sarafan*, while women in the south covered it with a skirt called a *ponyova*. A long apron might also be worn. Their footwear was also made of tree bark, felt, or leather. Young girls wore a single braid, while married women were expected to cover their hair with a scarf or hat. According to ancient beliefs, women's hair was thought to possess some special power that had to be restrained.

On holidays and other special days, Russian men and women wore their best clothing. The men's shirts might be elaborately embroidered. The women wore long shifts or shirts covered with sarafans or ponyovas, which were much more beautiful than their everyday outfits. Women embroidered the outfits and decorated them with ribbons and buttons. Various regions of Russia used particular colors for the basic fabric and for the embroidery thread. Favorite designs such as geometric figures, plants, animals, the sun, or birds, were used for embroidery. Women also used lace and crochet. On their heads women usually wore a *kokoshnik*, a kind of headdress or hat whose shape and size varied from region to region. Made of such fine fabrics as silk or velvet, the headdresses were decorated as richly as possible, with ribbons, metallic thread, glass beads, river pearls, and even jewels. Women might also have shawls, often of very high quality. The holiday clothing ensembles were so rich and took so long to make that they were frequently passed down from generation to generation.

Russian peasant dress changed little over the centuries, but this was not true of the upper class. Early in the eighteenth century, Peter the Great forced upper-class men to shave their beards and abandon their Russian clothing in favor of the type of clothing he had seen in Western Europe. From then on, the upper classes dressed following the fashions of upper-class Europeans.

MODERN CLOTHING

Today Russians dress very much like Western Europeans and Americans. In communist times, clothing was not a high priority of the government, and the quality of the goods on sale was not very good. Material was shoddy and the styles uninspiring. Young Russians sometimes went to great lengths to get items of Western clothing that seemed stylish to them, like American blue jeans, and they were very brand-conscious, preferring brands such as Levi-Strauss over less familiar kinds. The clothing mass-produced in Russia was usually a poor, simplified imitation of styles that had been popular in the West the previous year and did not carry the cachet that actual Western clothes did.

In the early years of communism, Constructivist artists like Varvara Stepanova and Lyubov Popova engaged in designing avant-garde textiles and clothes, but most of their designs remained on paper rather than becoming the style of the day. Later designers also faced production problems in translating their designs into actual clothes. The designers at the Central House of Fashion, the government agency in charge of clothing design, regularly saw their creations fall victim to the limitations of what could actually be produced at the factories. One designer who did make a mark in the late years of communism was Slava Zaitsev, whose work could compete with the best Western designers. But in general, Russians were very dissatisfied with the quality of clothing available to them.

After the fall of communism, good clothing was easier to get—at least in the major cities—but only at a high price which many could not afford. People tended to put outfits together as best they could. Men had never adopted the suit-and-tie uniform in large numbers, and today many still wear a casual shirt, pants, and jacket as their daily attire. Young Russian women dress carefully in the most fashionable way they can manage, and aim at a slimmer silhouette than was popular in Russia during communist days.

The world of high fashion has arrived in Russia, and not just in magazines like *Vogue* and in shops featuring the creations of Western designers. Some new Russian designers have been making a splash, among them Valentin Yudashkin, who designs colorful flamboyant clothes, rich in ornament and detail, and very expensive. Olga Moyseyenko's gorgeous coats, which resemble fur but are actually needlework, have won fame around the world. The top fashion model, a representative of the leading Red Stars model agency, is Tatyana Ettinger, who regularly appears at the Week of High Fashion in Moscow, a major annual fashion show that began in the mid 1990s. The fashions made by Yudashkin and Moyseyenko and modeled by Ettinger are out of reach for most Russians, but might inspire an infant clothing industry that will provide clothing more to the taste of ordinary Russians than what they had to wear during the long years of communism.

SUGGESTED READINGS

Chekhov, Anton. "Siren." In Avrahm Yarmolinsky, ed., *The Portable Chekhov*. New York: Viking, 1947.

Gogol, Nikolai. *Dead Souls*. Guilbert Guerney, trans. New York: Holt, Rinehart, and Winston, 1948.

Goldstein, Darra. *A La Russe: A Cookbook of Russian Hospitality*. New York: Random House, 1983.

Hilton, Alison. *Russian Folk Art*. Bloomington: Indiana University Press, 1995.

Papashvily, Helen, and George Papashvily. *Russian Cooking*. New York: Time-Life Books, 1969.

Russian Life magazine: for clothing see 1/94, 2/94, 11/96, 1/97; any issue for food.

Tolstoy, Leo. *Anna Karenina*. New York: Penguin, 1978.

Toomre, Joyce. *Classic Russian Cooking: Elena Molokhovets' A Gift to Young Housewives*. Bloomington: Indiana University Press, 1983.

Volokh, Anne. *The Art of Russian Cuisine*. New York: Macmillan, 1983.

Von Bremzen, Anya, and John Welchman. *Please to the Table: The Russian Cookbook*. New York: Workman, 1990.

"The Bronze Horseman," a statue of Peter the Great in St. Petersburg, is as well known to Russians as the Statue of Liberty is to Americans.

The Moscow Kremlin, where tsars were once crowned, is now the seat of the Russian government.

A building damaged during World War II, left standing as a memorial to the Battle of Stalingrad (now called Volgorgrad).

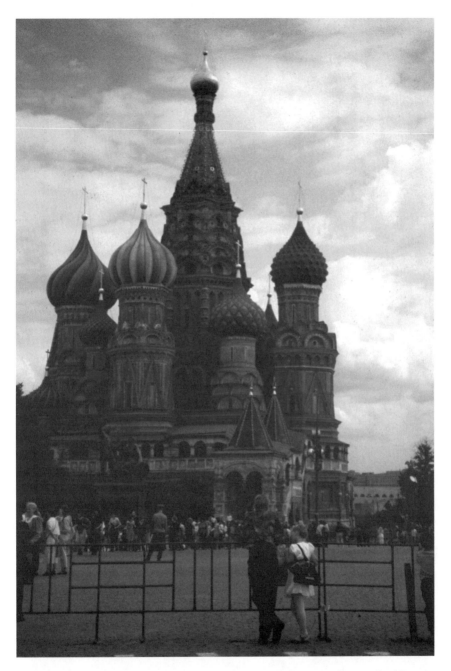

St. Basil's Cathedral on Red Square in Moscow is the most famous building in Russia.

Russian Orthodox Christians display icons—religious paintings—on a special icon shelf. This one is draped with handmade needlework.

Russian churches often feature distinctive domes, like these in the Kremlin.

These Russians have gathered for a group picture with a bride and groom in St. Petersburg.

Gorky Park is a favorite place to spend a free afternoon in Moscow.

One of several vendors selling vegetables, berries, and flowers on the sidewalk outside a grocery store in Uglich.

Russians are fond of Western imports like Pepsi and Coke.

Russians once poured hot water from samovars to dilute the tea they drank from cups or glasses. Modern samovars are electric.

Beautiful metal holders like these make it possible for Russians to drink hot tea from glasses.

This woman is dressed in a colorful native Russian costume.

Imagine racing across snowy fields wrapped in furs in your *troika* drawn by three horses.

A country house surrounded by birches, the favorite Russian tree.

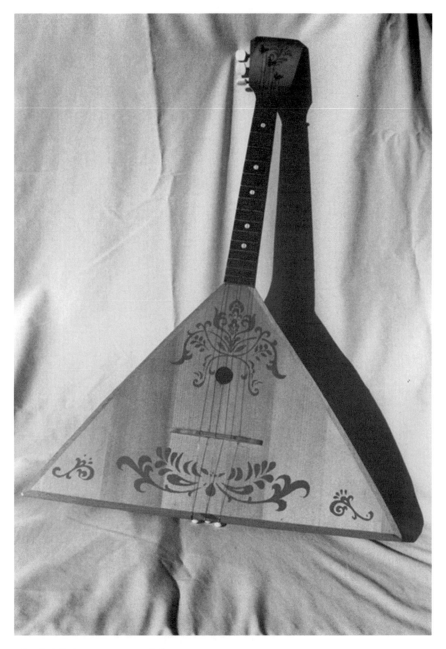

The *balalaika* is a Russian folk instrument.

These three young women in native costume perform traditional songs and dances.

A group of musicians relaxes after a performance.

The Hermitage in St. Petersburg is one of the greatest art museums in the world.

This woman continues the old tradition of lace-making.

This *matryoshka*, or nesting doll, shows Russian heads of state Lenin, Stalin, Brezhnev, Gorbachev, and Yeltsin.

Eggs are an ancient symbol of springtime and Easter.

Russian windows often have decorative wooden carving. The small pane, the *fortochka*, is used to let in fresh air.

This old log house is located in Irkutsk, a city near Lake Baikal in Siberia.

This beautiful wooden church in Kizhi was built without a single nail.

6

Literature

THE CLASSICS

RUSSIANS ARE EXCEPTIONALLY PROUD of their literature. Writers in Russia are traditionally the most respected and beloved members of society. Because of press censorship, literature is where the great ideas and issues facing the country have often been obliquely addressed, especially in the nineteenth century and to some extent in the twentieth century as well.

Until 1820, there was not much Russian literature of world-class quality. Russia produced an epic, *The Lay of Igor's Campaign*, and some tales and poems and plays, as well as chronicles and religious writing. Some of it is fascinating to read, but the very best writing appeared only in the last 200 years, most of it in a short sixty-year span.

The first great Russian writer, the Father of Russian Literature, Alexander Pushkin (1799–1837) sits at the pinnacle of Russian literature. Russians consider him not only their greatest poet but the greatest of all their writers in any genre, finer even than Leo Tolstoy or Fyodor Dostoevsky. Pushkin ushers in the Golden Age of Russian Literature (1820–1880), one of the most spectacular bursts of artistic creativity in the world history, similar to the golden age in Greece or the Italian Renaissance. The Russian contribution to world literature is their greatest gift to world culture, rivaled only by their music.

Pushkin is not as well known outside Russia as Tolstoy or Dostoevsky, primarily because most of his finest works are poetry, which is harder to translate than prose. His elegant, beautiful, deceptively simple language does not convey the proper effect in translation. Although few outside Russia are familiar with his masterpiece *Eugene Onegin*, most Russians can recite bits of it, and everyone knows the story. *Eugene Onegin* is a novel in verse, the story of Eugene, a bored young man who turns down the love of innocent young Tatyana, only to fall in love with her after she is a married woman in high society. She still loves him but will not leave her husband, putting duty ahead of love. Eugene is an example of a type in Russian literature called the "superfluous man," a person who because of the repressive regime cannot find a useful role in society. Tatyana is one of many "strong women" in nineteenth-century Russian literature, a literature as notable for its strong female characters as it is for its dearth of first-rank female authors during this period. Among the other characters in *Eugene Onegin* is Olga, Tatyana's flighty sister, and Lensky, Eugene's romantic young friend whom he kills in a duel. The story is told mostly in iambic tetrameter in special fourteen-line stanzas, known as Onegin stanzas, with the pattern ababccddeffegg. There are many beautiful sections, among them Tatyana's dream and her letter to Onegin. Pushkin's characterization, his plot development, his descriptions, and his commentary on contemporary life served as models for the famous novels that would follow.

Among Pushkin's many other long poems is *The Bronze Horseman*, which ranks nearly as high in Russian estimation. It is the story of another Eugene, a poor civil servant who during a great flood in St. Petersburg shows anger at the Bronze Horseman, a statue of Peter I (the Great). Eugene holds Peter responsible for building his city in a flood-prone area, keeping Eugene away from his beloved. The statue rears off its granite base and chases Eugene through the city; later Eugene is found dead.

Pushkin wrote many short poems, often about love, as well as plays and stories. His most famous play is *Boris Godunov*. Among his short stories, "The Queen of Spades" is the most memorable. In this story, Hermann tries to learn a secret to a card game as a means to amassing a fortune. In his zeal to learn the secret, he frightens an old countess to death; she later seems to sneer up at him as the queen of spades he has mistakenly placed his bet on instead of the winning ace.

Russians know all about Pushkin's life story as well. They know about his old nurse who taught him fairy tales: her picture has even appeared on a popular chocolate bar. They know about his problems with the censors, about his many love affairs, and about his fatal duel over his wife's honor when he was still fairly young. Squares, streets, even a whole town has been named after Pushkin, and it is not uncommon to see flowers placed at the foot of statues in his honor. Pushkin occupies the place in Russian literature that Shakespeare occupies in English literature, but the Russians feel a much more personal relationship, even affection, toward him than do English-speakers toward Shakespeare.

Mikhail Lermontov (1814–1841) is comparatively unknown outside Russia, but he is considered the finest poet after Pushkin and the author of the first novel of the realistic, psychological type that Russia became famous for in the nineteenth century. Lermontov's long poems include *Demon* and *Mtsyri* (The Novice). Although *Demon* has been more popular, *Mtsyri* is perhaps artistically superior. Set in the Caucasus Mountains, *Mtsyri* is the story of a novice, captured by Russians as a boy, who escapes the monastery in a doomed attempt to seek freedom and happiness in his native mountains. Lermontov's poetry is romantic, with lush descriptions and lonely heroes reminiscent of Byron.

Lermontov's novel *A Hero of Our Time* is essentially a set of five linked short stories. The main character is Pechorin, a superfluous man and Byronic hero in the mold of Eugene Onegin. Cold and calculating, Pechorin is nonetheless strangely attractive, not only to his acquaintances in the novel, but to generations of readers. The plotting, the descriptions, and the psychological analysis of Pechorin have made this novel a favorite. Shortly after completing the novel, Lermontov died in a duel; he was in his twenties.

Nikolai Gogol (1809–1852) is best known for his novel *Dead Souls*, his short story "The Overcoat," and his play *The Inspector General*. *Dead Souls* was conceived as a trilogy based on Dante's *Divine Comedy*, but the novel we have today represents only the first part of that trilogy. It is a comic masterpiece with a gallery of portraits of landowners that are well known to every educated Russian. Chichikov, the main character, visits these landowners to buy title to their dead serfs, for purposes that remain obscure for most of the novel. Much of the humor comes from his dealings with the landowners, each of whom represents a different type of personality, from sugary sweet to angry. Gogol is famous for his distinctive style, which is characterized by frequent digressions from the main plot and by long, unusual descriptions. His ornate style is often contrasted to that of Pushkin, which is a model of simplicity.

Gogol's story "The Overcoat" may be the most famous of all Russian short stories. The main character, Akaky Akakievich, is a very poor civil servant who needs to replace his worn-out overcoat to survive the harsh St. Petersburg winter. After much hardship, he finally gets the coat, only to have it stolen. Frightened by the important official he reports the theft to, he dies, only to return as a coat-stealing apparition. The story had a great impact on subsequent writers, who were attracted to its philanthropic theme and to its complex style.

For a time Gogol was mistakenly thought to be a liberal by critics for whom politics were the most important aspect of a writer's work and the criterion by which they judged writers. Gogol, however, was motivated less by politics and more by his vision of Russia's spiritual mission, which he wanted to convey in his work. His inability to complete *Dead Souls* with his grand vision contributed to his early death.

Ivan Turgenev (1818–1883) was the first Russian writer to become well known in Western Europe and America. He spent many years in Europe where he met famous writers and introduced not only his own works but those of other Russian writers to the outside world. Inside Russia, his works were politically influential. His *Sportsman's Sketches* (1852), a series of short stories set among the Russian peasants, gave an accurate portrayal of life among the serfs and had a great impact on the movement to abolish serfdom in Russia, similar to the impact Harriet Beecher Stowe's novel *Uncle Tom's Cabin* had on the movement to abolish slavery in the United States.

Turgenev's series of six novels gives an excellent picture of life in Russia from the 1850s through the 1870s, and is particularly strong for the 1850s and early 1860s. The first, *Rudin* (1856), gives a portrait of the liberals of the 1840s who talked a lot about reform, but never moved beyond the talking stage. The second, *A Nest of Gentlefolk*, gives an idyllic picture of life among the gentry (1859). The third, *On the Eve* (1860), shows that Russia is ready for reform, but questions whether there are Russian men to lead it. The hero of the novel is not Russian, but Bulgarian.

The fourth novel is Turgenev's masterwork and his most famous novel, *Fathers and Sons* (1862). *Fathers and Sons* became instantly famous for its portrait of Bazarov, who was meant to portray the younger generation of men in Russia who had no positive program of action for the country, but first wanted to clear the ground for future reforms. Largely as a result of this novel, they became known as Nihilists, from the Latin word for "nothing." They believed in science and had little use for literature, art, music, or any other trappings of civilization or tradition. In the early part of the novel, Bazarov has a great deal of influence over young Arkady Kirsanov, but gradually Arkady pursues his own path, while Bazarov, who has scoffed at romantic ideas of love along with all other traditional ideas, falls victim to love himself and eventually dies of an infected wound. Both traditionalists and radicals attacked the portrayal of Bazarov, and Turgenev fled abroad where he spent much of the rest of his life. His later novels *Smoke* and *Virgin Soil* are of lesser quality.

Turgenev also wrote several fine short works, including "Torrents of Spring" and "First Love." "First Love" tells the story of a young boy of sixteen who falls in love with the twenty-one-year-old woman next door. It is obvious she is in love with someone else, and he must grow up suddenly as he learns that it is his own philandering father she is in love with.

Turgenev's novels and stories feature beautiful language and sensitive characterization, but ultimately his reputation has been overshadowed by two giants of world literature who have dwarfed all other competition in the world of the novel. These two novelists, Leo Tolstoy and Fyodor Dostoevsky, are widely regarded as occupying one of the very highest pinnacles of literature, perhaps not as high a pinnacle as Shakespeare, but far above most other writers. In Russia, their reputation is second to Pushkin, but outside Russia, where Pushkin is relatively unknown, they rank at the top of Russian literature.

Fyodor Dostoevsky (1821–1881) is the Russian author who had the most profound influence on world literature in the twentieth century. In a century that stressed progress and social improvement, Dostoevsky explored the notion that people were fundamentally both good and bad, that they were irrational, and that they could not be assumed to act in their own best interest. He thought that in order for society to improve, people as individuals had to improve, and in his major works he stressed that Christianity was the path people should follow to that end.

Dostoevsky's work was profoundly affected by events in his early life. His father, an exceptionally unpleasant man, died under unusual circumstances, and although today we know that he was not murdered, all his life Dostoevsky believed that he had been killed by the peasants he had been cruel to. This gave rise to his interest in crime, especially murder, and in particular the murder of the father. His fits of epilepsy, which also play a prominent part in his works, began around this time. Another shattering experience also played a role in his psychic development. As a young man, Dostoevsky was arrested and sentenced to death for his participation in an underground political group. At the last moment, only minutes before he was to be shot, his sentence was commuted, and he was sent to Siberia instead. He recounted his experiences in his slightly fictionalized *Notes from the House of the Dead* (1862).

Dostoevsky's long story "Notes from Underground" (1864) laid the foundation for the series of four great novels on which his reputation rests. In

this work he explores the irrational behavior of an insecure man who be-
friends a young girl who has fallen into a life of prostitution, only then to
reject her. This work explores some of the themes Dostoevsky would develop
more fully in the novels that followed.

The first of his great novels is *Crime and Punishment* (1866). *Crime and
Punishment* is the story of a poor young student named Raskolnikov who
decides to murder a pawnbroker. His motives are murky: he wants to prove
that he is a superman capable of murdering without remorse, but he also is
in need of money. In committing the murder, he is forced to kill the pawnbroker's innocent sister who shows up at an inopportune moment. The rest
of the novel is taken up with Raskolnikov's punishment, which is more
spiritual than legal in nature.

The second novel is *The Idiot* (1868). Here Dostoevsky tries to create a
positive character in the mold of Don Quixote. The novel is quite complex
and is memorable for a striking murder scene. The idiot Myshkin meets his
dark double Rogozhin by the body of a woman Rogozhin has killed. The
third novel, *The Devils*, is also known in English as *The Possessed* (1872). In
this novel, which has a very complicated plot, Dostoevsky completes a devastating analysis of the young radicals of his time.

The fourth and final novel is Dostoevsky's finest work and the culmination
of his career. *The Brothers Karamazov* (1880) tells the story of the murder of
Fyodor Karamazov, the father of three sons, Dmitry, Ivan, and Alyosha.
Dmitry is his father's rival for the affections of the woman Grushenka and
is moreover in hot pursuit of money he thinks his father owes him from his
mother's estate. Ivan is a cold man, who has passed on his ideas to Smer-
dyakov, Karamazov's servant and possibly also his illegitimate son by the
village idiot. Alyosha is the saintly youngest son. Dostoevsky explores the
idea of who is actually responsible for the father's murder and who is morally
responsible. The most famous scene in the novel is the so-called Grand In-
quisitor scene, in which Ivan tells Alyosha a story about Christ's return to
earth during the time of the Spanish Inquisition, only to be rejected by the
Catholic Church, which, according to Ivan, had realized that people want
answers and security, not the freedom that Christ offered. In this his deepest
novel, Dostoevsky examines the meaning of life, the role of religion, and the
responsibility all humans have for one another.

Leo (Lev) Tolstoy (1828–1910) is considered by many to be the finest
novelist in world literature. His fame rests primarily on two books, *War and
Peace* and *Anna Karenina*, but his reputation was well established before he
published either work. The work that brought him notice was *Childhood*, a
short novel that was based on his own boyhood experience. This was followed

by short stories, in which he practiced his craft until he felt ready to write a long novel about Russia's great war against Napoleon and about the lives of the families involved in this great conflict.

Family life, war, and the meaning of life and death were to be main themes in his book, *War and Peace*. Tolstoy's life experience had prepared him well for this undertaking. He had thought hard about the importance of family life, since his mother died when he was only two and his father's death followed a few short years after. When he finally married his young wife Sonya, he was determined that his new family should be perfect. He had fought in the Crimean War and knew firsthand how soldiers felt in battle. He had experienced the death of both relatives and comrades and had thought seriously about life and death.

War and Peace (1869) is a sweeping epic, more than 1,400 pages long, which has as its centerpiece the story of Napoleon's invasion of Russia in 1812. The main character is warm-hearted Pierre Bezukhov, based on Tolstoy himself. The other main characters are lively, generous Natasha Rostov and Pierre's friend, the stiff and proud Andrey Bolkonsky. The book begins in 1805 and follows the fates of these and numerous other characters up through Napoleon's disastrous retreat from Moscow in 1812, then shifts forward in an epilogue to show the characters seven years later. The book concludes with an exposition of Tolstoy's philosophy of history, in which he puts forth the idea that ordinary people rather than generals and kings determine the outcome of battles. He also concludes that because our actions are influenced by everything that has gone before, we have only a very limited amount of real freedom to act as we please. Tolstoy's ideas are interesting and his descriptions of battle scenes are well done, but it is his ability to make his characters seem real that has made *War and Peace* the favorite book of so many people. The emotions and thoughts of the characters are so lifelike that the characters seem like people we actually know. It is amazing that Tolstoy can bring to life a young girl, a teenage boy, a cranky old aristocrat, a general, a grief-stricken old mother, even a wolf, with equal ease and success.

Tolstoy's other masterpiece is *Anna Karenina* (1877). This book tells the romantic yet tragic story of Anna, a beautiful young woman who falls desperately in love with Vronsky, a dashing army officer. Anna is married to an older man and has a young son on whom she has lavished all her love. She is torn between whether to stay in her marriage for the sake of her son or whether to run off with Vronsky. Their story is interwoven with the story of Kitty and Levin, whose relationship grows and prospers, while that of Anna and Vronsky eventually ends in tragedy. Just as in *War and Peace*, the characters are so vividly brought to life that they seem to leap off the page.

Particularly well drawn are Anna and her brother Stiva. Like Anna, Stiva is full of life, although unlike Anna, he can enjoy himself without worrying about the consequences of his actions. Also noteworthy is Tolstoy's use of dreams and symbols to heighten the feeling of doom that awaits Anna.

Tolstoy's other novel *Resurrection* (1899) is good, but not of the quality of the other two books. It concerns the spiritual resurrection of a man who caused a young girl's downfall, then found himself on a jury to convict her of a crime years later. Among his shorter works, Russians like to read Tolstoy's three Sevastopol tales, which give an accurate portrayal of the feelings of young men in battle, and his most famous short story "The Death of Ivan Ilyich," which analyzes the feelings of a man as he gradually comes to terms with the idea that he is going to die. His "The Kreutzer Sonata" has also received a lot of attention, especially since it was banned for a while. On the surface, it is about a man who kills his wife, but ultimately it is an attack on sex and marriage as damaging both to men and to women.

At the time of his death in 1910, Tolstoy was one of the most famous people in the world. His fame rested not only on his literary works, but on his activities as a moral and religious figure. During his long life, he had written extensively on religion and social issues and spoken out on many controversial topics. People wrote to Tolstoy from all over the world, and many came to see the great man on his estate Yasnaya Polyana. His reputation remains very high to this day, and every Russian knows his works. Many even travel out to Yasnaya Polyana to see where he lived and where he is buried.

The Golden Age of Russian literature ended in 1880, after the publication of *The Brothers Karamazov* and *Anna Karenina*. Yet one more great writer emerged at the end of the century. Anton Chekhov (1860–1904) is known primarily in the West as a playwright, but he began his career by writing funny short sketches to give him extra money while he prepared to be a doctor. Many Russians today still think of him as the author of these sketches. As Chekhov's writing career developed, however, he began to write many fine short stories, among them "The Lady with the Dog." This story is meant to comment on Tolstoy's *Anna Karenina*. Here, an ordinary young married woman falls in love with an ordinary man who is also married, and they try to find some happiness in their infrequent secret meetings. Unlike *Anna Karenina*, there is no sense of high drama or doom, just ordinary people trying to live life as best they can. Chekhov stressed that people should try to gain some happiness in life and should be bold in pursuing it. A product of an unhappy childhood in which he was frequently beaten, he spoke out against cruelty and was an exceptionally humane person both in his writings and in his dealings with other people.

TWENTIETH-CENTURY LITERATURE

With the death of Chekhov, the nineteenth century was finally over. During the early years of the twentieth century, there were many different types of writing, realistic, decadent, symbolist, and so on. Perhaps the finest novel of the first two decades was Andrey Biely's *St. Petersburg*, a symbolist novel about the conflict between the moribund old aristocratic Russia and the younger revolutionary generation, played out as a bomb attack on an old senator by his ineffectual son. There are many references to Russian literature of the past, including the Bronze Horseman, and the novel today appeals mostly to literary specialists.

The first two decades represent a Silver Age in Russian literature, largely because of the fine poetry written in that period. There were symbolist poets like Alexander Blok, who was perhaps the best Russian poet of this century. His best work is *The Twelve*, about a group of twelve revolutionary soldiers, with a Christ figure crowned in white roses at their head. Acmeist poets, who wanted to use more concrete imagery than the symbolists, included Osip Mandelshtam and Anna Akhmatova, widely acknowledged as the best female poet Russia has produced. Futurist poets, who wrote about airplanes and bridges and used odd typefaces and made up new words, were the most exciting group. Chief among them was Vladimir Mayakovsky, known as the Poet of the Revolution. His work includes poems that served the communist cause, such as "My Soviet Passport," but also many poems about his favorite subject, himself, including "An Extraordinary Adventure Which Befell Vladimir Mayakovsky at a Summer Cottage," in which he compares himself to the sun and invites the sun down to have tea with him. Official disapproval of Mayakovsky's late work, especially his plays, along with an unfortunate love affair, led him eventually to shoot himself.

The 1920s saw a flowering of short prose, resulting in the best decade for literature in the twentieth century. Typical was Yuri Olesha's short novel *Envy*, about the envy an imaginative but ineffectual man named Kavalerov has for the new Soviet man, whose big ambition is to create a cheap sausage to help get women out of the kitchen. Evgeny Zamiatin's novel *We*, a science-fiction dystopia satirizing communist regimentation, was so subversive it was never published inside Russia until the late 1980s. Its characters, D-503, O-90, and I-330, live in a society that can maintain its control over people only by performing an operation to remove their imagination. Fyodor Gladkov's *Cement* shows women's new independence, but indicates that creating a new society may demand the sacrifice of personal family happiness. While working to build a new Russia, the couple Dasha and Gleb Chumalov grow apart, and their child Nurka dies in day care.

The communist government made increasing demands on writers. Censorship under the tsars had meant that certain topics were to be avoided, but under communism, writers found that they were expected to write about certain approved topics in an approved style and with an approved political slant. The writers Ilya Ilf and Evgeny Petrov illustrated the effects of such censorship in their humorous work "How the Soviet Robinson Was Made." In the story, an author is writing about a Russian Robinson Crusoe, but his editor makes him add so many elements showing the positive effects of communism that the story is completely unrecognizable by the end.

In reality, it became not merely frustrating, but dangerous to write in Russia. During the 1930s, a doctrine called Socialist Realism was introduced, which forced writers to write according to a certain formula. Writers who did not comply, or who were simply considered suspect, were not published and could face prison camps or even death. The poet Mandelshtam was one prominent victim of the terror in Russia during this period. Some writers sought safety in other forms of writing, such as children's literature or film scripts, and others abandoned writing altogether. What had been one of the most exciting literatures in the world ten years earlier was now largely a wasteland.

During World War II, in an effort to whip up patriotism, some writers were allowed to publish once again. Akhmatova's poems began to appear after a ban of almost twenty years, but after the war when she was no longer needed, her work was denounced. She was expelled from the Union of Writers and lost her right to publish. Only after the death of Stalin in 1953 did literature regain a limited amount of freedom.

There were two great publishing events in the late 1950s and early 1960s. First, Boris Pasternak, after trying unsuccessfully to have his novel *Doctor Zhivago* approved for publication in Russia, saw his work appear in the West both in Russian and in translation. The Russian government forced Pasternak to reject the Nobel Prize, awarded soon after the publication of his book which had captured the world's imagination with its poetic depiction of Yuri Zhivago and his beloved Lara during the years of the revolution. Second, Alexander Solzhenitsyn's *One Day in the Life of Ivan Denisovich* appeared in 1962. This slim book details one ordinary day in the life of a simple man in a prison camp, the first time that the government had allowed the topic of forced-labor camps to be addressed in Russian literature. Solzhenitsyn followed this with more exposes in *First Circle* and *Cancer Ward*, but his work was no longer welcome for publication in Russia. Forced to emigrate, he continued his work in the United States in the 1970s and 1980s, producing most notably his account of prison camps, the multivolume *Gulag Archipelago*, which he had begun in 1958, and the opening parts of his huge epic, *The Red Wheel*, set at the time of World War I and the revolution. Solzhenitsyn was awarded the Nobel Prize for his work.

Late in the 1960s a novel appeared that had been written decades before, but was never published. Mikhail Bulgakov's *Master and Margarita* brought hopes that there would be a lot more "drawer literature" found, that is, literature which had been written and simply set aside in a drawer, because it would not be accepted for publication by the authorities. This did not prove to be the case, but the satirical *Master and Margarita* soon became a favorite with Russian readers, who wholeheartedly embraced the fantastic tale featuring a cigar-smoking cat, a Pilate who suffers from headaches, Christ and the devil, an author and his mistress Margarita.

During this entire period since the revolution, a second Russian literature existed, a literature written in emigration. Dozens of prominent writers left Russia around the time of the revolution, convinced that they could not continue writing in such an inhospitable environment. Many of them settled in Paris and Berlin, but they also settled in other major cities, mostly in Europe. Most of them remained in exile, although some returned later to Russia, sometimes with unfortunate results. The author of the standard history of Russian literature, Dmitry Sviatopolk-Mirsky, was arrested and sent to the camps where he disappeared. Among the best writers was the poet Marina Tsvetaeva, whose powerful poetry was often written under difficult circumstances, so difficult that she eventually committed suicide after returning to Russia. The first Nobel Prize ever given to a Russian went to emigre writer Ivan Bunin in 1933, in part to honor all the emigres. Bunin's most famous story "The Gentleman from San Francisco" predates the revolution, but his writing career spanned six decades and included many fine, lyrical works. The best-known emigre in the West is Vladimir Nabokov, who began his writing career in Russian with such masterpieces as *The Gift*, but later began writing in English as well. He became famous in the United States as the author of the notorious *Lolita*.

A new emigration began around 1970. Together with the willing emigres were writers like Solzhenitsyn who in earlier times might have been shot, but now were merely exiled from the country. Among these emigres was Joseph Brodsky, the poet who went on to win a Nobel Prize. Another was Vladimir

Voinovich, whose masterpiece is the amusing novel *The Life and Extraordinary Adventures of Private Ivan Chonkin*, which was refused publication in Russia but appeared in Paris in 1975. Georgy Vladimov's novel about a former prison-camp guard dog, *Faithful Ruslan*, was also published in the West about the same time. The author, who bravely not only resigned from the Writer's Union but illegally started up a branch of the human rights organization Amnesty International in Russia, left Russia in the early 1980s. Sasha Sokolov asked to emigrate and published his unusual novel *A School for Fools* in the United States with Ardis, a small but exceptionally important publishing venture begun by Ellendea and Carl Proffer in Ann Arbor, Michigan; Ardis rescued many twentieth-century works that could not be published in Russia.

When Mikhail Gorbachev finally assumed power in 1985, things began to change. The controls on literature were loosened and works that had previously not appeared legally in Russia began to be published openly. Writers (like Solzhenitsyn) who had been forcibly exiled and stripped of their citizenship, were welcome to come home. Readers avidly began catching up, reading works that might be well known in the West, but had circulated only clandestinely in Russia. They read *We, Doctor Zhivago*, Solzhenitsyn's novels, Nabokov. Andrey Platonov's *The Foundation Pit*, a satirical novel from the 1920s about people who are excavating a huge pit for a foundation for an ill-conceived massive building project, brought new luster to the name of this long-dead author. Vasily Grossman's *Life and Fate*, barred from publication in 1960, explored the oppressive communist system against the background of the battle of Stalingrad. Andrey Bitov's *Pushkin House*, a modernist novel about the disintegration of intellectual life in Russia, also appeared in print.

Anatoly Rybakov's *Children of the Arbat* caused a huge sensation when it came out. This novel followed the fortunes of a group of young people in Moscow as Russia descended into the terror of the 1930s when Stalin began his paranoid attempt to rid the country of any possible opposition. The psychological portrait of Stalin in the book is excellent, and the young people, especially Sasha and Varya, are well drawn. In subsequent years, Rybakov published two more parts of his trilogy, *Fear* and *Dust and Ashes*, bringing the history of Russia up into World War II. He used Sasha and Varya to show how Russia's finest young people suffered under Stalin and were swept away in the devastation of the war.

It must have seemed for a moment that Russia might be on the verge of a great new age, with a literature built on the combined rootstock of Soviet literature, banned literature, and emigre literature. It was very exciting reading the great literature that had so long been kept away from the people, in a land that placed authors on a pedestal unimaginable in other countries. But the opened floodgates that gave them *Dr. Zhivago* also allowed in everything else, including a great deal of trash from the West. Meanwhile the economy was faltering, and people had other concerns besides the state of literature on their minds. The journals that published so much of the literature began to have financial difficulties as interest waned, secure government support dried up, costs rose sharply, and the distribution system weakened. In any case, readers had depended on writers to give them the news about the moral health of the country, because censorship deprived them of frank discussions in the press. Now in the 1990s such discussions were possible, and the need for writers to serve as arbiters of the culture was diminished. People could read, for instance, *Argumenty i Fakty* (Arguments and Facts), a weekly newspaper which had the largest circulation of any newspaper in the world and was full of pictures and interesting tidbits in addition to opinions about life in Russia.

Some even said that literature was dead. But of course that was not true. Writers whose careers were underway before the breakup of communism continued to write, and new writers appeared, some of whom were excellent. Evgeny Evtushenko, the world-famous poet who became known as early as the 1950s, continued to be active, writing a novel *Don't Die before Your Death*, and Vasily Aksyonov, a youth idol of the 1960s, produced *Generations of Winter*, a major novel about the 1920s through the 1940s. It follows the fate of the Gradov family as they live through Stalin's terror and the war with Germany.

As can be seen from the descriptions above, a favorite topic in literature was the recapturing of the past, especially of the lost years when it was difficult to write openly about what was really going on in Russia. The disasters of industrialization and the collectivization of agriculture, the political purges of the 1930s, the devastating war with Germany, all were analyzed with a view to facing the horrors the Russians had lived through. In the 1990s, the Russian Booker Prize was established for the best works to appear that year. Mark Kharitonov won a Booker prize in 1992 for his postmodernist novel *Lines of Fate*, about a young researcher who tries to piece together an account of the past from candy wrappers a long-gone author wrote on, and Georgy Vladimov won for *A General and His Army*, an account of World War II and the secret police. Not all writers resort to the past. Vladimir Makanin, another Booker winner and a postmodernist, has written several short novels or novellas, focusing on contemporary problems like crime. His work is often surreal, set in alternate worlds or in the future.

One of the most promising young writers today and a great favorite with readers is Viktor Pelevin, who also resorts to the surreal in his work. His novel *The Life of Insects* features characters who turn into insects; in another work, the story "The Werewolf Problem in Central Russia," humans become werewolves. Best known is Pelevin's *Omon Ra*, a satire on the Soviet space program. Omon, who has always dreamed of flying, becomes a cosmonaut, only to find that his ultimate fate in the space program is not what he expected.

Some outstanding women writers have also emerged in today's Russia. Many tend to focus on problems of women. Ludmila Petrushevskaya, who is also a first-rate dramatist, in her work *The Time—Night* tells about the difficult life of Anna, who writes about romantic ideas in her notes, in contrast to the hard life of poverty she leads taking care of her sprawling and troubled family. Ludmila Ulitskaya also writes about everyday family life, but in a less grim fashion, in *Sonechka and Other Stories*. Tatyana Tolstaya produced two volumes of imaginative, beautifully written short stories, *On the Golden Porch* and *Sleepwalker in the Fog*, before turning to essays which have often appeared in *The New York Review of Books*.

Numerous other writers have published since the fall of communism. Among others well worth watching are Yuz Aleshkovsky, Alexey Slapovsky, Viktor Erofeev, Nina Sadur, Sergey Gandlevsky, Dmitry Prigov, Leonid Latynin, Valeriia Narbikova, Viktor Sosnora, Vyacheslav Pyetsukh, Evgeny Popov, Valery Popov, and Vladimir Sharov.

What will become of Russian literature in the twenty-first century? From a technical standpoint, Russian writers have always had high standards in the crafting of their prose and poetry. Traditionally, they have taken their mission to seek out the truth very seriously, and their social commitment is unmatched in world literature. Because writing is such a high and honorable calling in Russia, the profession of literature has attracted some of the best minds in the last two centuries. Whether that will remain true in this era of diminished importance for the writer in society is hard to predict.

POPULAR FICTION

From the late 1980s onward, Russians had access to a wide array of reading material, both foreign and Russian. In addition to new literature and literature that had been forbidden or long unavailable because of political considerations, Russians read a great deal of foreign popular fiction, everything from the crime novels of James Hadley Chase to the racy novels of Jacqueline Susann. They found new domestic favorites as well. At the top is Alexandra

Marinina, a former high-ranking official at the Moscow Law Institute who has done extensive research in the area of crime. She published her first psychological detective novel titled *A Concurrence of Circumstances* in 1993. The heroine is Anastasia Kamenskaya, a Moscow detective nicknamed Nastya. Since then, Marinina has written about twenty novels starring Nastya. Sales have been phenomenal, with more than 17 million copies in print. In 1998 she was named Writer of the Year. When her new novel *The Ghost of Music* was published early in 1999, the first printing of 250,000 sold out in ten days, despite the fact that Russians were still reeling from the collapse of the ruble only months before and had little money to spend on anything other than bare necessities. A television series called *Kamenskaya* was in the works at NTV-Kino, starring Elena Yakovleva. A popular magazine recently named Marinina to the list of twenty-five most influential people in Russia.

FAIRY TALES

Besides their great body of serious literature and their ephemeral popular literature, Russians have a world of folk literature in the form of fairy tales or *skazki*. Writers like Pushkin drew on these tales for inspiration as did such composers as Nikolai Rimsky-Korsakov. In the nineteenth century, many of these tales were collected by Alexander Afanasyev. It is estimated that the total number of tales available for collection was actually in the thousands, although many were variations on the same themes.

Just as most Americans know about Snow White or Cinderella, most Russians today know fairy tales like the story about Ivan, the Firebird, and the Gray Wolf. Ivan is the youngest of three brothers, a common motif in Russian stories, and he must bring back for his father the Firebird that has been eating his father's apples. On the journey he is helped by a Gray Wolf, who keeps giving him instructions which he disobeys. After many adventures in which he acquires the Firebird and a horse with a golden mane as well as the beautiful Princess Elena, he sets off to return to his father. Although he is killed along the way by his jealous brothers, Ivan is restored to life and ends up with the fair Elena.

The story about Vasilisa and her doll and the witch Baba Yaga who rides around in a mortar with a pestle is also a favorite. Vasilisa has an evil stepmother and stepsisters like Cinderella. She is given many hard tasks, but unlike Cinderella does not have to actually work hard because she has a doll given to her by her mother on her deathbed who does the work for her. Sent to Baba Yaga on a contrived errand by her sisters, Vasilisa arrives at Baba Yaga's house, a hut that stands on chicken legs and is surrounded by a fence of human bones and skulls. With the aid of her doll and some common sense Vasilisa survives the visit, and in the end it is her sisters who suffer rather than Vasilisa. Often in Russian fairy tales the youngest girl or boy, who is considered stupid or is picked on in some other way by older siblings, ends up successful. In these stories having to work hard is not necessarily a virtue; being able to get the work done without lifting a finger was no doubt much more attractive to the hardworking people who invented the stories.

Russians know many other stories, like the one about the Frog Princess or the one about the Seven Semyons. Russian children grow up with these stories, as well as many more modern children's works by authors such as Samuel Marshak or Korney Chukovsky, part of nearly every child's upbringing, and a link with the far distant Russian past when fairy tales were first told.

SUGGESTED READINGS

Afanas'ev, Aleksandr. *Russian Fairy Tales*. New York: Pantheon Books, 1973.

Mirsky, D. S. *A History of Russian Literature*. New York: Alfred A. Knopf, 1966.

Moser, Charles, ed. *The Cambridge History of Russian Literature*. Cambridge: Cambridge University Press, 1996.

Terras, Victor. *A History of Russian Literature*. New Haven, CT: Yale University Press, 1991.

$$7$$

The Media and Cinema

TELEVISION

RUSSIAN TELEVISION was once strictly controlled by the state. Experimental transmission began in 1931 and the first centers in Moscow and Leningrad were functioning in 1938, but television use really began to grow after World War II. Russia had 10,000 sets in 1950 and nearly 3 million in 1958. In the late 1950s, television was on about four hours a day, and more than half of all shows were live. Russian films were released to TV as early as ten days after they were shown in the theater and made up 40 percent of the telecasts. Russians also got music, sports, theater, news, and children's programs, all without commercial interruption because everything was state-sponsored.

In the next decades, television use continued to spread. Eventually most Russians, even in the countryside, had access to television in the years under communism. Televisions were not very expensive, and they were fairly plentiful. In the mid 1980s, sports programs were a great favorite with the viewers, especially soccer and ice hockey, as were foreign films. There were also cultural shows featuring opera, ballet, folk dancing, and folksinging. News shows were carefully constructed to present the correct ideological slant. As the political situation in Russia began to change in the mid-1980s, new, more entertaining shows like police dramas began to appear, but in general in the communist era, there were few options for viewers who were looking for an evening of light diversion.

Now, however, the situation is quite different. After communism fell, a large number of Western shows, especially American shows, flooded the airwaves. As the century drew to a close, Russians could watch *Beavis and Butthead, Sesame Street, Star Trek, Dynasty, Melrose Place, The Simpsons, Rocky and Bullwinkle, Beverly Hills 90210, Falcon Crest, Sunset Beach, Cagney and Lacey, Alf,* and *Grace under Fire.* The French show *First Kisses, Rich and Famous* from Argentina, and *Marielena* from Spain were also playing, as well as shows from England. Most appeared in their original form, but *Sesame Street* was unusual in that it was re-created especially for Russian children, in a joint-venture project that took five years and cost millions to develop. *Sesame Street,* or *Ulitsa Sesam* as Russians call it, appeared in the Russian version with some new characters like Zeliboba, Businka, and Kubik, although Bert and Ernie made appearances as Vlas and Enik. *Ulitsa Sesam* was set in a Russian courtyard rather than on an American street. As might be expected, American movies like *Halloween III* were also widely watched on television, in addition to the various series.

Russians were also making their own television shows, many of them similar in form to Western shows. Russians had their choice of morning shows, but the original one, *Good Morning* on station ORT with the prominent news anchor Larisa Verbitskaya, had been a favorite for more than a dozen years. The words *sitkom* and *tok shou* (talk show) entered the language, and Russians developed versions of both. The first Russian sitcoms, such as *Funny Business, Family Business,* and *Strawberry Café,* aired in 1997. The talk show *I, Myself* had topics like "Well, what am I to blame for, daughter?" Elena Hanga's talk show *About This* aired after midnight because of its adults-only content. The show *My Family* covered topics like "Are family and career compatible?" as well as racier topics. Vladimir Pozner, who once appeared regularly on American television to talk about Russia, hosted the show *Person in a Mask,* which featured people who appeared in masks for very good reason. One guest was a KGB (secret police) agent as well as a mafia drug king responsible for seven murders. Crime victims also appeared. Game shows were also popular. *Field of Miracles* with host Leonid Yakubovich, a show similar to *Wheel of Fortune,* enjoyed great success on station ORT. Among other shows were *Dog Show. My Dog and I, Sign of Quality* for those who wanted to show off their talents; several crime shows like *Petrovka 38* and *Road Patrol* and *Criminal; Happy Birthday,* with astrological predictions for those celebrating their birthdays; and *Buy!, Good Night, Kids, Guess the Melody,* a game show *Call of the Jungle,* the "romantic-psychological" show *Love at First Glance,* and *Motor Club. Big Money* was a highly regarded program on economics. There were shows on homeopathy, health issues, and the weather, as well as cartoons, films, fashion, cultural shows, sports, and music shows. Russia aired soccer matches, tennis matches, and other sports.

When a special match between soccer teams such as Dinamo and Zenit or Torpedo and Spartak aired in the evening, the regular show *Good Night, Kids* might play at the half. There were other kinds of special shows as well. On New Year's Eve, the main holiday of the year, a very special telecast on ORT was watched by millions. Russia also produced some very interesting documentaries, such as one on Afghanistan.

In 1999, the major television stations were ORT, RTR, and NTV. ORT, the government station formerly known as Ostankino, became a semiprivate holding company in 1994. It aired *Good Morning, Sesame Street, Field of Miracles*, and *Person in a Mask*. RTR showed *Love at First Glance* and *My Family*, and NTV had the show *Dog Show*. NTV was independent; the other two were state-sponsored. Other channels at the end of the century included TV6, TV-Center, Kultura, Moskovia, Tele-Expo, TNT, 31 Kanal (Channel), Ren TV, Muz TV, STS, MTV, TV Stolitsa (Capital), and TV 3. Kultura showed films, ballet, art discussions, and classical music. STS specialized in American series like *Melrose Place*. MTV, based on the American MTV, first went on the air in 1998. On MTV, viewers could watch their favorite VJ, Tutta Larsen, complete with nose ring and bleached hair, play videos from Russian and foreign bands. MTV also aired *Beavis and Butthead*. There were also satellite channels NTV Plus and Kosmos TV. NTV Plus had films, cartoons, sports, and adult material. Kosmos TV accessed sports, BBC, Nickelodeon, and numerous other channels.

In communist times, news and information shows were closely scrutinized, and even today, television stations tend to be more careful about the political implications of what they broadcast than their American counterparts. When controls began to loosen before the fall of communism, Russians could already watch with fascination Alexander Nevzorov hosting *600 Seconds*, which showed them, in ten very fast-paced minutes, such scenes as police dragging bodies out of rivers. His show exposed petty scandals such as a communist official's efforts to secure a Mercedes for himself. *View* (*Vzglyad*) also showed Russians new things, for example, interviews with KGB agents or soldiers who had fought in Afghanistan. At the very end of the communist era in 1991, the government under Mikhail Gorbachev began tightening the censorship on news shows as the empire began to crumble. For instance, when antigovernment violence broke out in Lithuania, censors prohibited a news anchor from broadcasting the truth about what was happening and rewrote her script. She was replaced by a stand-in when she angrily refused to read the altered script on the air.

Boris Yeltsin was well aware of the power of television and used it to advantage. On the eve of the election in 1996, the airwaves were saturated with shows designed to paint the communist opposition in a bad light. On election eve, the movie *Burnt by the Sun* was shown on television, reminding viewers of Stalin's reign of terror in the 1930s, when so many innocent Russians were murdered at his order. Even more recently, supporters of rival politicians in Russia complained about the overwhelming good press given Yeltsin on news programs, particularly on the state-owned stations, but also on stations owned by Yeltsin sympathizers. Yet there is certainly more freedom on television than there was under communism. During the first Chechen conflict, a state television station infuriated Yeltsin by reporting that his orders to his commanders were being ignored. The station representative later stated that its loyalty lay more with the people than the authorities. One enormously popular show on television was based entirely on political commentary on the news. *Kukly* (puppets) was a highly amusing satire on current political figures, using puppets to represent people like Yeltsin and Bill Clinton. In one hilarious episode, Yeltsin gives Clinton advice about how to take care of television stations that air news he does not like. Yeltsin cannot understand why Clinton frets about being caught lying and reminds him that he is Commander-in-Chief, with tanks at his disposal. In this satire on Clinton, the show is of course making very pointed comments about Yeltsin himself. One early episode, which showed Yeltsin and other Russian politicians trying to live on the tiny pensions allowed retired people, made such an impact on viewers that it caused the authorities to investigate the show. Not surprisingly, the effect was to increase the show's popularity. *Kukly* was conceived for the independent station NTV by Vasily Pichul, better known as the director of the film *Little Vera*.

Television has come far in forty years, from a time when only one in twenty had access to television to a time when nearly everyone watches it. In that time, television has changed from being a sober purveyor of heavily censored news and cultural material to a bouncy combination of trash and entertainment and news and a little of everything else. Once there was no advertisement, but now viewers can see ads for everything from fortune-tellers to the tax service, which has advertised on television using cartoons to persuade people to pay their taxes. Once television was seen as a medium for promoting communism, but it is just as effective in promoting an open society, which explains why those attempting to overthrow the government seek early on to control television transmission. When a coup was attempted in 1991, tanks surrounding the television center at Ostankino, to control what went over the air. In 1993, when a struggle for power broke out between Yeltsin and the Duma, Yeltsin's opponents tried to seize Ostankino, which was defended by troops. Both times the attackers were successful in blacking out the news, but only for a short time.

Television has created popular personalities known to all Russians. The best-known of these was Vladislav Listyev, who appeared on *Vzglyad* and *Field of Miracles*, as well as on *Rush Hour* (*Chas Pik*) and *The Theme*, all of them audience-participation and interview shows. He eventually also became general producer of ORT. A powerful and beloved figure, he was assassinated in 1995 for reasons that remain unclear, although there was speculation that it had to do with money deals that were somehow threatened by his position as producer. The public outpouring of grief was greater than at any time since the death of Stalin in 1953. Both the assassination and the grief over Listyev's death confirmed the power that television had acquired in Russian life.

Just as in the West, television in Russia at the end of the twentieth century was the premier source of instant news and entertainment, far outdistancing radio, movies, and newspapers. Whether the computer would challenge that position was a question for the future.

NEWSPAPERS AND MAGAZINES

Russians have a variety of magazines and newspapers to choose from. *Playboy, Elle, Cosmopolitan*, and *Reader's Digest* are all available in Russian editions. *Speed-Info* is a popular tabloid full of gossip about stars, fashion, secrets about nature, and other items of casual interest. *Megapolis Express* provides the latest gossip, and *Profile* reports on secrets and intrigues among the power elite. Magazines directed primarily at women include the best-known magazine for women *Rabotnitsa*, or *Worker*, with information on recipes and fashion, as well as *She* and *Hearth*. *Amadeus* gives men news about music and film, and *Bear* tell them about topics such as women, gambling, clubs, weapons, and hunting. *Sport Express* provides sports news. Several magazines are devoted to health, with such titles as *Home Doctor* and *Women's Health*. *Family*, published for over a hundred years, is a magazine aimed at parents. Some publications focus on a narrow subject: *World of the Criminal* explores aspects of crime both foreign and domestic; *Auto* and *Behind the Wheel* are for car buffs; the biweekly *Computerra* has advice on computers; and *Premiere* is for information on film, videos, and Western TV. *Science and Life* gives news from the field of science, and the biweeklies *Power* and *New Time* focus on political news. Two of the most famous publications are known in English by their Russian names: *Itogi*, which is similar to *Time* or *Newsweek*, and *Ogonyok*, which has long been a favorite source of news and articles of all sorts, including politics and culture. Among newspapers, besides the weekly *Arguments and Facts*, people read several others, including the respected *Kommersant*. The venerable *Literary Gazette*, usually known in English by its Russian name *Literaturnaya Gazeta*, continues to publish news from the world of literature and culture.

CINEMA

Movies were being made as early as 1895 in the West and by 1896 were being shown in Russia. At first they were a novelty shown at music halls and fairs, usually by traveling projectionists. The first Russian feature film, *Stenka Razin*, was made in 1908 and was less than eight minutes long. Stenka Razin was a real person who led a peasant uprising in the seventeenth century and is the subject of a well-known folk song. In the film, his men trick Stenka into believing that a captive Persian princess has been unfaithful, and he throws her overboard into the Volga.

By the onset of war in 1914, movies, 90 percent of them imported, were the most popular form of entertainment in Russia. The flow of imported movies was drastically reduced by the war, and by 1916 most movies that Russians saw were being produced inside Russia. Viewers could watch comedies, adventure films, and costume dramas, but most popular were the psychological melodramas, often about young girls who came to a bad end after getting involved with the wrong type of man. Some of the best films made were versions of literary classics like *Anna Karenina*, *Crime and Punishment*, and *The Queen of Spades*. In the short decade before the communists nationalized the cinema, independent Russian filmmakers produced about 2,000 films.

In August 1919, a year and a half after the communist revolution, Vladimir Lenin signed an order nationalizing all aspects of the production and exhibition of films. Lenin realized the power of film and considered it the most influential of all the arts. Trains with short propaganda films were sent all around the country to educate people about the new regime. At first, times were very hard for filmmakers. Half the filmmakers emigrated, and those that remained found film stock in short supply. But by the mid-1920s, Russia was enjoying a golden age of film. Among the pioneers was Dziga Vertov, creator of Kino-Pravda, or film-truth, the newsreel or documentary. Vertov experimented with splicing film, learning how to create special effects like reversing time, showing a loaf of bread that gradually goes back to being a stalk of wheat. Another experimenter was Lev Kuleshov, who became a master of montage, or arranging bits of film to create a certain effect. Kuleshov learned that by juxtaposing a clip of a man's face with a bowl of soup, he could convey hunger, while if he juxtaposed the same clip with a coffin, he could convey grief. Kuleshov learned some of his techniques by studying the work of the American filmmaker, D. W. Griffith. Among Kuleshov's best-known films is *The Extraordinary Adventures of Mr. West in the Land of the Bolsheviks*, a comedy about an American in Russia. Kuleshov is also remembered for setting up a formal training program for film actors. Another note-worthy early director was Kuleshov's student Vsevolod Pudovkin. Pudovkin's best films are *Mother, The End of St. Petersburg*, and *Storm over Asia (The Heir to Genghis Khan)*, all lyrical studies of individuals and their involvement with the revolution.

The best and most famous of all Russian directors was Sergey Eisenstein. During the Golden Age of 1925–1929, he completed four films: *Strike, The Battleship Potemkin, October (Ten Days That Shook the World)*, and *Old and New*. All have fine examples of montage, of which Eisenstein was Russia's best practitioner, but the most spectacular and successful example in any of his movies is the Odessa Steps scene in *The Battleship Potemkin*, which itself has been called the best film ever made. The movie portrays the 1905 work-ers' revolt by focusing on the events on one ship, where the sailors mutiny. Toward the end of the film, tsarist soldiers fire on civilians who have turned out in support of the sailors. The film shows the soldiers marching inexorably down the long steps at the seaside in Odessa, killing innocent men, women, and children. In a famous part that has been copied and even parodied in recent films, a baby carriage goes rolling down the steps. Eisenstein cuts back and forth between the soldiers and the victims, with many close-ups of faces and of significant detail. Even though the film is in black-and-white and is silent, the scene is still gripping after seventy-five years. Eisenstein's early films do not have a single hero or stars, but try to use the mass of humanity as the main character.

While these great films were being produced and exhibited, the public was spending more time at lighter, more popular films. *The Bear's Wedding*, a movie about a vampire, was the biggest box-office success of the period. Western films with such stars as Mary Pickford also did very well, and the Russians even made a movie about a pair of star-struck Russians called *The Kiss of Mary Pickford*. Another popular film was *Aelita*, a science-fiction movie with costumes by the artist Alexandra Exter.

As Russia descended into a period of terror under Stalin, it became dan-gerous to make controversial films. Some entertaining films were produced, like *Chapayev* and *Volga, Volga*, and sound was introduced, but great films were few. After a stint in Hollywood, Eisenstein returned to make *Alexander Nevsky*, about the thirteenth-century prince, and *Ivan the Terrible*, a beautiful film tracing the rise of Ivan, a strong leader and consolidator of Russian power in the sixteenth century. His sequel, *Ivan the Terrible Part II* ran into difficulties with Stalin, because it showed the leader's doubts about himself and therefore seemed to be a commentary on Stalin. It was released only years after Stalin's death.

In the late 1950s, two movies set during World War II gained worldwide respect. *Ballad of a Soldier* shows how terrible war is by focusing on the fate of one young soldier, and *Cranes Are Flying* focuses on a young woman on the home front. In the 1960s, Sergey Bondarchuk directed the twelve-hour Academy Award–winning epic *War and Peace*, a faithful rendition of Leo Tolstoy's novel set during the time of Napoleon's invasion of Russia. This decade also saw the work of female directors, such as Kira Muratova, who made *Brief Encounters*.

Andrey Tarkovsky's impressive *Andrey Rublev*, based on the life of Russia's greatest icon painter, appeared in 1969. Over the next decade, Tarkovsky made *Solaris*, *The Mirror*, and *Stalker* before going into exile because of differences with the communist government. He is considered one of the best directors Russia has produced since Eisenstein. The charming *Slave of Love*, about movie making early in the century, and the Academy Award–winning *Moscow Doesn't Believe in Tears*, which follows the lives of three young women, also appeared during this same period. Two other movies that became audience favorites were *White Sun of the Desert*, an adventure film, and *Irony of Fate*, a romantic comedy about a man who wakes up New Year's morning in an apartment just like his, but in a different city. Today in Russia it is a tradition to watch *Irony of Fate* every New Year's Eve. In the West, movies had suffered a decline with the onset of television, but movies were still very popular in Russia, which had the highest attendance per capita in the world. *Moscow Doesn't Believe in Tears* sold 75 million tickets, a record.

During the 1980s, as communism began to break down, movies that had been banned or shelved by the government for various reasons began to be released. Films that dealt with corruption, family breakdowns, or despair and were therefore not acceptable to the censors could now be shown. Directors like Kira Muratova and Alexander Sokurov, who had had difficulties with the government, could make films again. Directors became bolder and began to explore contemporary social problems in their films. One of the best was Vasily Pichul's *Little Vera*, an enormously popular film about disaffected working-class youth, starring Natalya Negoda, who later appeared in a *Playboy* spread.

The 1980s seemed at first like the beginning of a renaissance for film, given the new era of openness in the later years of communism. This promise was only partially fulfilled in the 1990s. A number of good films were made. Pavel Lungin directed *Taxi Blues*, a bleak critique of life in Russia, and *Luna Park*, a film about a gang of skinheads. On the lighter side was *Adam's Rib*, which told the story of an overburdened woman's attempts to take care of her mother and daughters, while dealing with her ex-husbands and looking for romance. Yuri Mamin's *Window to Paris* told the fanciful tale of a man who finds that he can go directly through an opening in his drab Russian apartment and end up in colorful, bountiful Paris. *Prisoner of the Mountains*, based on a story by Tolstoy about a Chechen father who wants to exchange two Russian prisoners for his captive son, was nominated for an Academy Award. Vladimir Khotinenko's award-winning films *Makarov* and *The Moslem* both examine the crisis of the soul in modern Russia. All these movies comment on problems facing Russia at the time, among them shortages, the war in Chechnya, crime, despair, and intolerance. There was also an abundance of cheap, poorly made films about sex and violence.

In the mid-1990s, it was apparent that the Russian film industry was in crisis. After the initial euphoria at the downfall of communism in 1991, Russians as individuals faced the reality that their economic situation was precarious. Retired people found that inflation left them very poor. Many working people lost their jobs, or went for months without pay. Millions were forced to do whatever they could to feed their families. Many could afford neither the time nor the money to go to the movies, nor were they in the mood to see movies about problems facing Russia. In late 1996, a group of theater managers, sociologists, and film distributors gathered to discuss the precipitous decline in movie attendance. They noted several problems besides the mood and economic condition of the patrons. Filmmakers could not make technically sophisticated films because they did not have the proper equipment; few theaters had advanced systems like Dolby sound to make the most of projecting the films. The quality of the film prints was poor, in any case. The distributors did not get the films delivered to outlying regions. Distributors might provide only one small poster for advertising purposes and then ask for its return after the showing. Advertising on television would be more effective, but was too expensive. The bottom line, though, seemed to be that people had lost the habit of going to the movies. The real problem was that television was too great a competitor, now that state control had loosened and the shows were more pleasing to the audiences. And if people wanted to see a movie, videos were now available. The group concluded that they needed to lure new audiences, by means of better quality films shown on big screens with better equipment. They were divided on whether the government should help with organizing the effort to achieve these goals.

At least one effort was already underway, however, but it was in private hands. The NTV television company and the Igor Tolstunov production company founded a film production and distribution company called NTV-Profit in 1995, backed by MOST Bank, which also backed NTV, radio stations, newspapers, and magazines. NTV-Profit has backed several films, including Muratova's *Three Stories*, three separate tales linked by the theme of violent death; Denis Yevstigneev's *Mama*, based on a true-life plane hijacking; Vladimir Mashkov's *Sympathy Seekers* (*Kazan Orphan*), a Christmas tale about a girl searching for her father; Alla Surikova's *I Want to Go to Prison*, a comedy about a man who schemes unsuccessfully to get arrested and sent to a luxurious Dutch prison in order to avoid a Russian one. The best-known film backed by NTV-Profit was Pavel Chukhrai's *The Thief*, a film set in the aftermath of World War II about a boy and his mother, who are charmed by a man who turns out to be a common thief instead of a handsome, gallant army officer. This film was nominated for an Academy Award, and won several other prizes, including a Nika, the Russian Academy Award, in five different categories. Like many Russian directors, Chukhrai was educated at VGIK, the All-Union State Institute of Cinematography, and had experience in other areas, in his case camerawork, before becoming a director of feature films.

Other efforts were being made to attract customers. For instance, Kodak's new movie theater Kinomir in central Moscow attracted customers with its excellent sound and projection equipment. The Union of Russian Filmmakers turned away from the experimental filmmaking of the 1980s and elected Nikita Mikhalkov, the most celebrated director in the new Russia, to lead them back to making films that would draw the public with their universal appeal, movies that would show respect for Russians, their history and culture. Russians could be attracted to good movies, as shown by the crowds that turned out for the American film *Titanic* at Kinomir, even at prices that were double the usual. Mikhalkov is best known for his beautiful Academy Award-winning film *Burnt by the Sun*, an understated, lyrical, but ultimately horrifying study of Stalin's reign of terror in the 1930s. Mikhalkov stars as the revolutionary hero who becomes Stalin's victim, and his daughter Nadya plays the general's small daughter. In 1999, his movie *The Barber of Siberia* opened in Moscow to a star-studded premiere in the Kremlin attended by thousands of people, including Prime Minister Evgeny Primakov and Communist leader Gennady Zyuganov. The movie, designed for worldwide appeal, stars both Russian and Western actors, including Julia Ormond, and much of the dialogue is in English. It is a love story set a hundred years ago and features an American with plans to harvest the forests of Siberia with a huge machine he has invented. Financing for the $45 million film came mostly from business, with $10 million from government funding. The film was shown in Moscow to audiences at the same time that *Pleasantville, Parent Trap*, and films starring Adam Sandler and Jackie Chan were playing, as well as a few Russian movies.

Some are hopeful that Russian cinema is turning a corner and will regain its former position in Russian life. Russia has a long distinguished tradition of filmmaking, with many world-class films to its credit. Once an extremely popular form of entertainment, movies will perhaps recover to some extent as they did in America after the initial onslaught of television, or perhaps their best days lie in the past. What happens depends as much on the mood of the country, influenced by its economic condition, as it does on the accomplishments of the film industry. Now that the industry is market driven rather than enjoying full state support, the audience is more important than ever.

SUGGESTED READINGS

Leyda, Jay. *Kino: A History of the Russian and Soviet Film*. New York: Collier, 1973.

Stites, Richard. *Russian Popular Culture: Entertainment and Society since 1900*. Cambridge: Cambridge University Press, 1992.

Zorkaya, Neya. *The Illustrated History of the Soviet Cinema*. New York: Hippocrene Books, 1991.

8

The Performing Arts

CLASSICAL MUSIC

RUSSIA IS WORLD FAMOUS for achievements in two cultural areas, literature and music, both of which had their golden ages in the nineteenth century. The father of Russian classical music was Mikhail Glinka (1804–1857), who set the pattern for golden age music by combining elements borrowed from Western music with Russian folk music, church music, and Russian stories to create a new form of music that fit well within the Western tradition but was at the same time distinctly Russian in content. His opera *Ivan Susanin* tells the story of a Russian peasant, Ivan Susanin, who sacrificed his own life by leading the enemy Poles astray in order to save the life of the tsar, Mikhail Romanov. Glinka renamed the opera *A Life for the Tsar* after the tsar attended a rehearsal. Today it is known by either title. His other great work, *Ruslan and Ludmila*, based on Pushkin's poem of that name, features fairy-tale characters. Glinka's orchestral work *Kamarinskaya*, which uses tunes from Russian folk weddings, like his other works greatly influenced subsequent composers.

Mily Balakirev, a disciple of Glinka, founded a group of composers that was known as the Balakirev Circle, the Five, or the Mighty Handful or Kuchka. The members of the group were Balakirev, Cesar Cui, Modest Musorgsky, Nikolai Rimsky-Korsakov, and Alexander Borodin. The five, following Glinka's lead, wanted to use Russian folk and religious music in their compositions. The group also intended to ally themselves with the more modern music of composers such as Chopin and Liszt rather than classical composers of previous generations. Although they both wrote fine music,

Balakirev is remembered first for his role in forming the Five, while Cui is remembered for his music criticism and for promoting the work of the Five. Borodin is famous for his opera *Prince Igor*.

The most creative of the group was Musorgsky (1839–1881). All these composers were nationalists, promoting the idea of Russia in their music, but Musorgsky was the greatest nationalist of all. His music departed freely from established forms and used folk music and themes. He is also known for his preference for realism over romanticism. Author of eighty songs, Musorgsky is considered the greatest Russian song writer. Of his long pieces, one of the best known is *St. John's Night on Bald Mountain*, or simply *Night on Bald Mountain*. Near Kiev there is a mountain that is the legendary site where once every year spirits and witches and other creatures assembled to revel and pay homage to the devil at a witches' sabbath. Musorgsky's tone poem evokes that night. After Musorgsky's death, Rimsky-Korsakov edited the work, and this is the version that was often performed rather than Musorgsky's original version. Leopold Stokowski also did a version that many know from its performance in Walt Disney's *Fantasia*. Rimsky-Korsakov also reworked Musorgsky's opera *Boris Godunov*, based on Pushkin's play. Rimsky-Korsakov made Musorgsky's piece more conventional, less dissonant, and more palatable to listeners of the time. Equally well known is Musorgsky's *Pictures at an Exhibition*, written in honor of his late friend Viktor Hartmann and an exhibition of his art. Musorgsky wonderfully portrays in music ten pictures, such as Baba Yaga's hut, the great gate of Kiev, and chicks in their shells, as well as his own heavy tread as he lumbers through the exhibition. Originally intended as a work for piano, the composer Ravel later adapted it for orchestra, and it is heard in both versions today.

Nikolai Rimsky-Korsakov (1844–1908), the youngest of the group, was not as original as Musorgsky but was much more influential. He not only wrote music, but orchestrated the works of other composers. He also taught several musicians who became well-known composers, such as Alexander Glazunov, Igor Stravinsky, and Sergey Prokofiev. Rimsky-Korsakov's *Scheherazade* with its lush romantic melodies is familiar to most listeners. Of his fourteen operas, *Snegurochka*, *Sadko*, *The Golden Cockerel*, and *Tsar Saltan* are especially popular. *Snegurochka*, the story of a snow maiden who melts into a spring torrent, contains the familiar "Dance of the Tumblers," and *Sadko* contains the "Song of India." The well-known "The Flight of the Bumblebee" is from Rimsky-Korsakov's *Tsar Saltan*.

The best known and most beloved of all Russian composers is Pyotr Tchaikovsky (1840–1893). His music is beautiful, full of gorgeous melodies in a wide variety of styles. His first great work was *Romeo and Juliet*, based on

Shakespeare's play. He wrote eleven operas, of which the best known are *Eugene Onegin*, based on Pushkin's novel in verse, and *The Queen of Spades*, based on Pushkin's story. He composed three famous ballets, *Swan Lake*, *Sleeping Beauty*, and *The Nutcracker*, which he also reworked as a suite based on the ballet. *Swan Lake* is probably the most famous of all ballets. The music from *Sleeping Beauty* is perhaps more familiar to Americans from its extensive use in the Disney movie. Tchaikovsky's enormously successful ballet *The Nutcracker* is often performed today at Christmas time in American cities. The wonderfully familiar tunes from *The Nutcracker* evoke various nationalities and moods. Tchaikovsky was never fond of his *1812 Overture*, commemorating the victory over Napoleon and incorporating music from that time, as well as booming cannons, but it has remained a favorite with listeners. Connoisseurs sometimes rate Tchaikovsky's 6th Symphony, the *Pathétique*, as his masterpiece, and indeed the masterpiece of Russian music as a whole. The mood of *Pathétique* is somber, but gathers force before descending finally into a deathlike silence. Tchaikovsky was depressed at the end of his life as he wrote this piece, perhaps partly caused by the withdrawal of his long-time patron, correspondent, and friend Nadezhda von Meck, whom he had never met in person, and who may have learned his secret— that he was homosexual. Only a few days after the premiere of his *Pathétique*, Tchaikovsky died under suspicious circumstances, possibly either from cholera contracted from drinking unboiled water, or from drinking arsenic.

In the twentieth century, no one has matched the appeal of Tchaikovsky, although there have been some excellent composers. Sergey Rachmaninoff, one of the greatest of all pianists, is best known for his Second Concerto in C Minor. The composer Alexander Scriabin turned to pantheism and mysticism for inspiration and created a color organ to project rays of light to correspond to the sounds of his modernistic music.

Igor Stravinsky (1882–1971) is perhaps the greatest Russian composer of the twentieth century. He became associated with the entrepreneur Sergey Diaghilev, who engaged him to compose for the Russian ballet, the Ballets Russes, which Diaghilev was mounting in Paris beginning in 1909. Stravinsky wrote the ballets *The Firebird, Petrushka*, and *The Rite of Spring* for the performances of the Ballets Russes. The modern music marked a great change from the music of the previous century and at first mystified and disturbed and amused some of the dancers and musicians. *The Firebird* was based on a Russian fairy tale about a magic bird with bright plumage; *Petrushka*, which incorporated many familiar Russian songs, was about a puppet who comes to life only to be killed by a rival. Both pieces were successful and brought Stravinsky recognition as a composer. *The Rite of Spring*, which uses harsh dissonance and pounding rhythms, was at first much more controversial. In this work, Stravinsky attempted to portray pagan fertility rites, including a young maiden dancing herself to death as a sacrifice to the god of spring. The Paris audience at the premiere erupted in boos, the police were called, and one Paris newspaper played on its French title *Le Sacre du Printemps* and called it *Le Massacre du Printemps*. Yet soon *The Rite of Spring* was recognized as a true masterpiece, a landmark in the history of music and ballet. Stravinsky stayed in Europe during World War I, first becoming a French citizen and then moving to the United States. His constantly evolving and exceptionally creative work continued to make use of Russian sources, although from that point onward he ceased to be a purely Russian composer.

Sergey Prokofiev and Dmitry Shostakovich are regarded as the best Soviet composers, that is, composers who lived and wrote in Russia during the Communist period 1917–1991. Prokofiev spent the years 1918–1933 in the West, but before and after that time he lived in Russia. Prokofiev studied under Rimsky-Korsakov, and like Rachmaninoff, was an excellent pianist. He wrote the *Classical Symphony*, the ballet *Romeo and Juliet*, the opera *War and Peace*, the music for Sergey Eisenstein's film *Alexander Nevsky*, and numerous other works, among them the children's favorite, *Peter and the Wolf*. At one point, Prokofiev was criticized by the authorities for writing music that was too dissonant, but he was soon back in favor. Shostakovich also incurred official disfavor, in his case for his opera *Katerina Izmailova*, also known as *Lady Macbeth of the Mtsensk District*, based on a story by Nikolai Leskov. In far greater favor was his Seventh Symphony, the *Leningrad*, inspired by the siege of Leningrad during World War II. This symphony became a symbol of the defense of Russia during that great moment in history. The Eleventh Symphony, the *1905*, was composed to mark the fortieth anniversary of the 1917 Revolution. It shows how the workers lost their faith in the tsar after the slaughter of peaceful protesters, thus preparing the way for the revolution. His Thirteenth Symphony, the *Babi Yar*, was based on a poem by Evgeny Evtushenko about the massacre of Jews by the Nazis at Kiev during World War II.

Composers were expected to conform to certain principles of composition under communism. They were supposed to stick to traditional music forms and avoid experimentation. Two recent composers, regarded as the best composers of their generation in Russia, had difficulties with the authorities because of their music. The very prolific Alfred Schnittke composed nine symphonies, several concertos, ballet scores, and other works. He composed scores for more than sixty films, an occupation that provided much of his income. Schnittke's manner of composition is often referred to as polystylistic, because he chose to work with a wide variety of styles rather than limit himself to one. His disregard for officially approved methods put many roadblocks in his career until the loosening of restrictions under Gorbachev after 1985. In poor health after a stroke, Schnittke moved to Germany in 1990, retaining dual citizenship. His reputation growing, he continued to compose. His work won numerous prizes and received wide acclaim in the West as well as in his native Russia, where he was given a major award the year of his death, 1998.

Sofia Gubaidulina also chose a path that displeased the authorities. Encouraged to continue to develop along her own "mistaken" path by Shostakovich at her graduation from the music conservatory, she mastered Western methods but also studied unusual Russian, Caucasian, and Asian instruments, which she uses in her compositions. She became deeply interested in the spiritual and mystical aspects of music. Because of her unusual music, for a long time she was not recorded and seldom performed. Like Schnittke, she turned to writing film scores for income. Her work gained recognition outside Russia in the 1980s, and her reputation has been growing ever since. Among her works are *Offertorium, Hour of the Soul*, and *Two Paths. Two Paths*, about Martha and Mary in the Bible, had its world premiere in New York in 1999. In some of her work, Gubaidulina explores the ideas of the feminine and the masculine, as in her *Hour of the Soul*.

The standards of performance in Russia traditionally have met the high standards of the music itself. Russia has a long line of distinguished conductors, musicians, and singers. Today Russia continues to maintain that high standard. The most-talked-about conductor in the world in the late 1990s was Valery Gergiev of the Kirov orchestra in St. Petersburg. Named artistic director of the Kirov opera at the young age of thirty-five in 1988, he was faced with little financial support and the loss of many musicians who fled to the West, where they joined orchestras that could pay them a living wage. Nevertheless, he was able to augment his orchestra with young musicians and singers just out of school, and he began touring the world with them to earn money to support the group. Within ten years, the Kirov was as highly regarded as any opera house in the world. Gergiev also began recording a long series of Russian operas, symphonies, and ballets to universal acclaim. His recordings have brought new recognition to works such as Rimsky-Korsakov's *Legend of the Invisible City of Kitezh*. Recently he has mounted productions of Glinka's *Ruslan and Ludmila*, Prokofiev's *Betrothal in a Monastery*, and Borodin's *Prince Igor*. As a side benefit of Gergiev's work, new Russian opera stars like Galina Gorchakova and Olga Borodina have emerged.

In the new Russia, it became possible for individuals to organize orchestras not sponsored by the state. In 1990, the Russian National Orchestra became the first private symphony orchestra in Russia since the revolution in 1917. The group was assembled by the pianist and conductor, Mikhail Pletnev. The group has recorded fine versions of Rachmaninoff, Prokofiev, and Tchaikovsky for the prestigious Western firm Deutsche Grammophon.

SONGS

Folk songs were a staple of peasant life for centuries. Because the main job of peasants was growing crops, many of the songs were calendar songs, tied to the growing season and sung at certain times of the year. The growing year began with the return of the sun at the winter solstice. Groups went door to door singing and asking for treats, and if they got good treats, they sang a song promising their hosts a good harvest. As winter faded, there were songs encouraging spring to come and other songs about various plants and crops. Calender singing went on until the summer solstice, and then picked up again at the harvest. Not all songs were agricultural. There were songs about hauling barges, soldier songs, and even robber songs and prison songs. Another very large group of songs had to do with love and marriage. Russians sang love songs and songs about faithless lovers or lovers separated by their families. The songs of single girls tended to be cheerful, while women's songs at the time of marriage and thereafter tended to be unhappy, which reflected the hard life of women in patriarchal Russia.

In the nineteenth century, several writers and composers became interested in folk songs. For instance, Pushkin incorporated one into his poem *Eugene Onegin*. Balakirev, Rimsky-Korsakov, and Tchaikovsky used them in their compositions. Turgenev's story "The Singers" in his book *Sportsman's Sketches* very vividly portrays the contest between two peasant men to see who can sing better.

A few of these old songs have survived into the present, not just as part of a collection in some book, but as songs that people still sing. They have joined other more modern songs in a repertoire of songs that most people know and sing when they get together for a social gathering. Everyone can join in to sing "Kalinka," a lively song about love under a snowball bush. Another favorite is "Katyusha," about a young woman who takes care of their love while her man is off defending the country. "The Volga Boatman" is frequently sung. "Moscow Nights," which was a hit in the West as well as in Russia, is a more modern favorite.

Russia also has a tradition of gypsy songs and of church music. Because there are no instruments in Russian Orthodox church services, singing has always played an essential role. In the last several years, there has been renewed interest in many forms of traditional music, and both professional and amateur groups have sprung up to perform it both in Russia and abroad. These groups tend to be less slick and homogenized than the official groups sent to tour the West in communist times. For example, a folk group made up largely of factory workers and teachers and others who sing in their spare time toured the United States in the late 1990s. Dressed in traditional outfits, some of which they made themselves, they presented authentic songs and dances passed down through the generations.

FOLK INSTRUMENTS

Russian folk music uses some instruments that are not well known in the West. The quintessential Russian instrument is the *balalaika*. The balalaika is a bit like a guitar in shape, but the main body is triangular. It has three strings and comes in various sizes. The balalaika can be played with a pick or with the fingers and sounds a little like a banjo, but richer. Balalaikas have been used for at least three hundred years.

The *garmon* is similar to an accordion, as is the *bayan*, which is more complex than the garmon. Since its development in the early twentieth century, the bayan has become more widely used than the garmon.

One of the oldest and most popular instruments, the *gusli* was used as early as the sixth century. The name is said to come from the "goo" sound it makes. The gusli is a stringed instrument that once came in two types, the winged gusli with 5–12 strings and the helmet gusli with 11–36 strings, both of which were held on the lap. About 400 years ago, floor and tabletop gusli with 55–66 strings were introduced. Today, helmet gusli are no longer used.

The *domra* was played in the sixteenth and seventeenth centuries, fell out of use, and was revived in the nineteenth century. It looks a bit like a banjo and comes in various sizes and tones, such as bass, tenor, and alto. It can have three or four strings.

The *zhaleika* is a kind of horn-flute that curves up at the end, about 5–8 inches long. It is often made of wood and makes a sharp, plaintive sound when blown. Another curved horn with holes is the *rozhok*, which is 12–32 inches long.

Russians also play with a set of three to five wooden spoons, called *lozhki*, to which bells may be attached. Finally, there is the *svirel*, a set of two simple flutelike tubes, one about a foot long and the other about 18 inches. Each has three holes in the side.

In the nineteenth century, the musician Vasily Andreyev founded the first orchestra of folk instruments and personally perfected some of the instruments. Russian composers had made use of various folk instruments in their compositions, but there had never before been a whole orchestra devoted to them. In the twentieth century, several more folk orchestras were founded and achieved a certain popularity. One popular ensemble today, Bely Den, features vocalists as well as a domra, a balalaika, a guitar, and percussion instruments.

POP AND ROCK

Pop music and rock are enormously popular in Russia. The singer and songwriter Alla Pugacheva is as well known and instantly recognizable in Russia as Elvis or the Beatles were in America. On giving her an award for service, Boris Yeltsin told her that he would likely be remembered as someone who had lived in the era of Pugacheva. She has sold more than 100 million records in the past twenty years and has been called not just the most popular singer in Russia, but the most popular person. In performance, she is electric, capturing the crowd with her gorgeous soulful voice and fiery red hair. Her tempestuous private life is almost as interesting to her fans as her love songs. Articles about her appear frequently in the press, a book has been written about her, and a film called *A Woman Who Sings* featured her in the starring role. Recently a five-part television documentary recounted the story of her life. She has won numerous awards and has a long list of recordings, which are quickly snapped up by her many Russian fans.

The other noted singer of modern times is Vladimir Vysotsky, who died in 1980. Alla Pugacheva enchants audiences with her fire and free spirit, but Vladimir Vysotsky moved people with his raspy, heartfelt songs about world troubles. Vysotsky, a poet, wrote more than 600 songs, and also acted in movies. It was the social commentary and satire in his songs that made the government consider him subversive, but people circulated typed versions of his works and tapes among themselves and were devastated when he died. On the anniversaries of his birth and death, people visit his grave with flowers and candles. As beloved as Vysotsky, Bulat Okudzhava was a bard for a generation of Russians beginning in the late 1950s. One of his most famous songs is "Midnight Trolleybus," a song familiar to every Russian. Other noted singers of modern times are Alexander Galich and Alexander Rozenbaum. Some newer singers are Diana, who has won awards and toured abroad, and Leonid Agutin, whose popularity has been helped by his excellent TV video clips.

Today in Russia music of the *estrada* or stage, like Alla Pugacheva's, is very popular. Other forms of music, such as jazz, have a following as well. But the music of the younger generation is rock. The Russian language has adopted dozens of music terms used by English-speakers into Russian, and many of them are rock terms. Among words familiar to English-speakers are disc jockey, deejay, ambient, trance, swing, blues, jazz, combo, bandleader, rock and roll, rocker, reggae, punk, soundtrack, big-band, ska, rap, bootleg, country, beat, fusion, compact disk, label, drive, video clip, tour, remastering, single, album, nonstop, rockabilly, club, revival show, pop, hit, heavy metal, hard rock, boogie, musical, front man, dance pop, folk rock, sampler, rave, funk, soul, sample, house music, techno, industrial, producer, show business, leader, track, glam rock, disco, promotion, release, and real audio. Russian DJs sometimes have names that are just Russian spellings of English words, such as Spider, Smile, Groove, and Astral. Some of the clubs have names like Beverly Hills, Hungry Duck, New Relax, Riverside, Manhattan Express, and Taxman. Some rock groups have had such names as Time Out, and Cross-roads.

Rock has been associated with the English language since the beginning. In the 1960s, young Russians were mad about the Beatles and learned to sing the songs in English. Rock took Russia by storm, and tapes of rock songs, which could be fairly easily reproduced because many private individuals had tape recorders, passed rapidly from one young music fan to another. At first, rock music stayed in the underground, since such music was hardly likely to be approved by the government.

Eventually Russian groups began to compose music in Russian rather than just performing foreign songs. Since they operated outside the official sphere during the communist years, there was no opportunity to be a commercial success and gain great riches like Western rockers. Most rockers had other jobs and did not associate their commitment to rock with money. Rockers felt that their music could be purer and less commercial without the injection of money. Rock was also a male preserve, which it has largely remained to this day. A few groups have some female members, but not many.

Rock moved into the open in the 1980s but soon encountered difficulties. Music had been a conduit for the expression of alternative social ideas, but with the new era of glasnost under Gorbachev, opinions could be expressed in many other ways. With the fall of communism, rock groups theoretically should have been able to charge a lot for tickets for performances and record profitable tapes with whomever they wished, but in practice, there were severe problems. Inflation and financial problems of all sorts plagued them. Rampant piracy and lax copyright enforcement meant few profits from tapes.

Corruption and mafia interference in many aspects of Russian life did not help either. Faced with such difficulties, some young performers even considered tapping Western markets by performing in English and billing themselves as international rockers rather than as Russian.

Despite the many problems, Russian rock remains enormously popular. In 1998, *MTV Russia* (*Musikalnoe Televidenie*) hit the air with popular VJ Tutta Larsen, ready to show the top Russian and foreign videos. The hottest band at that time was Mumy Troll, who had played in the 1980s, then disbanded and reformed in 1996. Russians also listened to various radio stations for their favorite music. One station was 106.8 FM from Moscow, home of DJ and music editor Dmitry Korotkov, called Kor. Kor had also worked at such Moscow clubs as Gippopotam (Hippopotamus), X-Dance, Galaktika, Titanik, Robotek, and Megadance and organized a rave, when they were all the rage. Some other popular DJs were Zmey (Snake) and Zorkin. Many cities have clubs and discos, and the capital Moscow has dozens. In 1999, young people might want to go to Niagara, or the Ritz, or Utopia, or the Sports Bar, Armadillo, Jacko's Bar, Bulgakov, La Bamba, the Lucky Pizza Club, the Alexander Blok, or the A Club. The Beverly Hills sported a restaurant with California, European, and Old Russian cuisine, as well as a casino with Black Jack and, of course, music. Women sometimes got cheaper admission than men.

There are scores of well-known rock groups. DDT had trouble with the authorities in the early 1980s for the sharp antigovernment satire in their music. In 1993, they won an Ovatsiya, a Russian Grammy, as best rock group of the year. In 1995, they went on a peacekeeping mission to Chechnya and gave concerts heard by both sides in the conflict between Russians and Chechens. The group Lyube, which appealed to adults rather than teens and was known for songs about ordinary people's thoughts and feelings, recorded an album called *Kombat* dedicated to the war theme that was a hit at the time of the first conflict in Chechnya. Teen idols in the 1990s, the band Agata Kristi (Agatha Christie), named for the English mystery writer, recorded the very popular album *Opium*. Akvarium (Aquarium) was founded in the early 1970s by the best known of all Russian rock figures, singer and songwriter Boris Grebenshchikov, BG, and his friend, Anatoly (George) Gunitsky. Over the years the group experimented with many styles, including hard rock, punk, reggae, and new wave, among others. They were still very active in 1999. Grebenshchikov also performed solo. A recent album of his is called *Lilith*. Alisa's singer and songwriter Kostya Kinchev was behind much of his group's success throughout the 1990s. Auktsyon has roots in ska, reggae, and several other traditions. This popular group took part in the

"Rock of Pure Water" tour, playing in cities along the Volga to promote a clean environment. Mashina Vremeni (Time Machine) was important in the early transition from English to Russian rock music and remained popular in the 1990s. KINO has also been around for a long time. Nautilus Pompilius had a huge year in the late 1980s and has remained a top group. Pep-si was named in hopes of getting Pepsi sponsorship, but Pepsi took a dim view of the idea. The group, popular in the mid 1990s, had female singers, brought in by the two male performers and organizers of Pep-si. Other popular groups are Krematory (Crematorium), called Krem for short; Chizh; Chaif; Serga; Splin; and Mashi i Medvedi (Masha and the Bears).

Russian pop and rock have moved onto the Internet. Russians can consult a rock, pop, and jazz encyclopedia; read about Alla; find information about DKs (dance clubs) and new albums; and find out where to get an official "piratsky video bootleg" of the latest Mumy Troll concert, at discount if the ticket stub from the concert is presented. Some groups like Krematory even have Websites. Russians can hear music on the Internet and have welcomed the arrival of MP3.

DANCE

Russian folk dance, like folksinging, goes back many centuries. In modern times, dance troupes have taken folk dances from many areas of Russia and adapted them for professional performance. The most famous of these troupes is the Folk Dance Ensemble, better known as the Moiseyev Dance Company or Moiseyev Ensemble after its founder, Igor Moiseyev. Moiseyev, a classically trained dancer, formed the group in 1937, and since then, it has gained worldwide recognition. Some of the steps the male dancers make are immediately recognized as Russian. The Russian men crouch down, cross their arms and kick outward, first one leg and then the other. Or they may leap impossibly high in the air, legs and arms spread wide. The women's steps are traditionally less energetic. Recently there has been a movement to preserve the folk dances in their original forms. Groups in villages and towns across Russia gather to sing and dance in traditional costumes, preserving the old songs and dances learned from their parents and grandparents. Musicologists interested in the old ways also have formed groups to preserve traditional dances. The groups range from the far north city of Arkhangelsk to Rostov-na-Donu, where an ensemble is busily preserving old Cossack dances.

The best-known form of dance from Russia is not really Russian in origin. Ballet was imported from the West in the eighteenth century and was already popular by the time of Pushkin, who mentions the ballerina Istomina in

Eugene Onegin. In the early nineteenth century, Charles Didelot came from France to St. Petersburg with the intention of creating a ballet company as good as that in Paris. He wanted his rigorously trained dancers to be able not only to dance well, but to convey emotion and characterization through their dancing. He also paid attention to the staging of his productions, which could be quite elaborate. He and his successors began to make some use of Russian folk dancing and Russian stories in developing their ballets. All these would later become hallmarks of Russian ballet: the use of Russian materials, the elaborate sets, the extensive training, and the attention paid to character development.

As ballet waned in the West, its popularity in Russia grew steadily. Many of the dancers were trained in St. Petersburg, at the Imperial Ballet School. Although there were many applicants to the prestigious school, only the very best were selected for the training program which lasted several years. The students received the finest of care and at the end of their training began their dancing career, to the delight of the appreciative Russian audience.

The greatest of the nineteenth-century ballet masters was the Frenchman Marius Petipa, who came to St. Petersburg as a young man and stayed there the rest of his life, bringing Russian ballet to a peak of perfection during his forty-year reign at the top of what became the world center of ballet. Petipa was an excellent choreographer, introducing new steps, reviving old ballets and creating new ones. He combined the grace of classical French ballet with the Italian strength in acrobatics, the whole suffused with Russian flair and passion, to create a characteristically Russian form of ballet. Petipa was very prolific, responsible for forty-six ballets, including *Don Quixote, La Bayadère, Sleeping Beauty*, and *Raymonda*, and with Lev Ivanov, *The Nutcracker* and *Swan Lake*. *The Nutcracker* and *Sleeping Beauty* achieved fame partly due to the incomparably beautiful music of Tchaikovsky, but also because of the inspired staging. Many of his ballets are still performed today.

Of all the ballets in the world, *Swan Lake* is probably the one most familiar to modern audiences. In the story, a prince is out hunting and sees swans, who are actually maidens who have been turned into swans by an evil sorcerer. They can be freed only by a pledge of true love to the swan maiden Odette. Although the prince is willing to make the pledge, he is deceived into making it to the wrong woman, Odile, instead. In the original ending, the prince and Odette throw themselves in the lake to be united in the afterlife, rather than having a happy ending on earth as happened in communist productions.

Petipa's work appeared at the Mariinsky Theater in St. Petersburg, named after Tsar Alexander II's wife Maria. During communist years it was called the Kirov, after a communist leader of that name. The Mariinsky remains one of the two great ballet theaters of Russia, the other being the Bolshoi (Big) Theater in Moscow.

After Petipa, Mikhail Fokine, widely considered the founder of modern ballet, took over. He advanced the art of male dancing and introduced more comfortable costumes, under the influence of Siamese dancers and the American Isadora Duncan, who danced barefoot in flowing garments. Fokine's most famous creation was the role of the Dying Swan, immortalized by Anna Pavlova, probably the best known of all Russian ballerinas.

In 1909, Fokine was asked to join Sergey Diaghilev's Ballets Russes in Paris. The Ballets Russes was perhaps the most spectacular ballet production of all time, combining the entrepreneurial skills of Diaghilev with the talents of Fokine, the designers Leon Bakst and Alexander Benois, the composer Stravinsky, and the greatest dancer of all, Vaslav Nijinsky. Fokine created the ballets *Le Pavillon d'Armide* and *Les Sylphides*, as well as the Polovtsian Dances for *Prince Igor* for the opening season of the Ballets Russes. He then worked on *Scheherazade, The Firebird, Le Spectre de la Rose*, and *Petrushka* for the Ballets. All these are among the top ballets ever produced and were a great success in Paris.

The costumes and sets for the Ballets Russes deserve special mention. Bakst's luxurious designs in shades of blue and green for *Scheherazade* influenced styles in fashion and design for years to come. Women's draped skirts, turbans with feathers, and ropes of pearls, and perfumes like Shalimar owe much to *Scheherazade*, as do fringed lampshades and oriental cushions. Benois was responsible for the designs of several ballets, including *Petrushka*.

Many famous Russian dancers participated in the Ballets Russes. The reigning ballerina of a few years earlier at the turn of the century, Matilda Kshessinska, did not go to Paris, but Tamara Karsavina did go, creating the lead female roles opposite Nijinsky in *Petrushka* and *Firebird*. Anna Pavlova danced in *Le Pavillon d' Armide* and *Les Sylphides* with such success that she went on from Paris to create an independent career on stages all around the world, including the United States, where she danced in *Giselle* at the Metropolitan Opera House in 1910. The greatest of the male dancers was undoubtedly Nijinsky, who not only danced but choreographed as well. Nijinsky's dancing was flawless and his characterization impeccable. His awe-inspiring leaps where he actually seemed to hover in the air were unparalleled. He shocked some with his scandalous costumes and unconventional choreography, but he set a new, much higher standard for male ballet. Particularly noteworthy were his *Petrushka*, his erotic *L'Après-midi d'un Faune*, and his choreography for *The Rite of Spring*, with its angular frenzied jerks conveying the raw violence of spring, so unusual and so modern that the audience erupted and the police had to be summoned. This performance was a peak in the history of ballet that has perhaps not been equaled since. Nijinsky's career was cut short by mental illness. The Ballets Russes stayed in the West and influenced the development of Western ballet over the next decades. The Ballets Russes became more international, but some of the Russians associated with it during that time included Nijinsky's sister Bronislava Nijinska; Léonide Massine, who replaced Nijinsky as a dancer and later was known for his choreography; the dancer Alexandra Danilova; and the famous choreographer George Balanchine, who went on to found what became the New York City Ballet.

Meanwhile in Russia, ballet continued to develop along a more traditional path during the years under communism. Standards were quite high both for dancing and for sets and costumes, although innovation was not encouraged. The world's attention was once again drawn to Russian ballet when the great Bolshoi Ballet began performing in the West after the death of Stalin. Two great female dancers of communist times were Galina Ulanova and Maya Plisetskaya, who performed together as Odette and Odile in *Swan Lake*. Three dancers, Natalia Makarova, Rudolf Nureyev, and Mikhail Baryshnikov, came to instant fame when they defected during tours and went on to successful careers in the West.

From Nijinsky and Pavlova to Nureyev, Makarova, and Baryshnikov, many of the greatest dancers in Russia have trained at the Vaganova Academy in St. Petersburg, founded in 1738 and long considered the finest ballet school in the world, even better than the Bolshoi Academy in Moscow. Agrippina Vaganova, a ballerina, taught at the Academy for three decades after the 1917 revolution and published an influential book on her dance method that was a landmark in the history of dance. Today at the academy, only fifty students are admitted every year out of thousands of applicants. They receive rigorous training in dance, as well as an excellent education, graduating at seventeen. The best graduates may dance for the Mariinsky, or perhaps one of the dozens of other ballet companies in Russia. The Mariinsky company is huge, with about 250 members, and their productions are lavish. Russians of all types are fond of ballet and attend performances to a much greater extent than Americans.

The post-1991 period has been hard on ballet. Financial problems have plagued ballet just as they have every other aspect of cultural life. Some dancers have left to dance in the West; others have gone on tour with their companies in the West to earn money to supplement their earnings at home. The Bolshoi underwent a major upheaval in the 1990s when the man who had served rather autocratically as artistic director for thirty years, Yuri Grigorovich, resigned under pressure and was replaced by Vladimir Vasiliev, dancer and partner of prima ballerina Ekaterina Maximova. Vasiliev attempted reform in various areas, including increasing dancers' salaries and providing opportunities for dancers to earn more money by dancing independently. He also led an effort to add newly staged ballets to the traditional repertoire. Despite its troubles, Russian ballet has a long tradition of excellence. Its ballet remains different from American ballet, which emphasizes speed and innovation over the beautiful poses and traditional movements important to the Russians. Now that the walls have come down, it will be interesting to see what course the Russian ballet takes, and whether it someday will once again take the world by storm as it did already twice in the twentieth century.

THEATER

Russian theater has a long and illustrious history. Although there were earlier dramatic performances, the person who really got professional Russian theater underway was Fyodor Volkov, whose acting company began performing in the capital in 1752. Two prominent playwrights of the late eighteenth century were Alexander Sumarokov and Denis Fonvizin, author of the comedy *The Minor*. By the nineteenth century when Russian authors produced many masterpieces that are still regularly performed, the theater was already well established.

The first great Russian play was Alexander Griboedov's *Woe from Wit*, sometimes translated as *The Trouble with Reason*. The comedy, which is written in verse, has many memorable lines that Russians still use in their everyday speech. The main character Chatsky is an early example of a type that would become known as the Superfluous Man, a man of talent who cannot find a useful place in society. Chatsky returns to Moscow from his travels abroad to find that everyone around him is backward and petty and that his beloved Sofia is in love with someone else. Many funny characters in the play, among them Sofia's father Famusov, her beloved Molchalin, and Repetilov, are well known to all educated Russians.

Most of the famous Russian writers of the nineteenth century wrote plays, including the greatest of all Russian writers Alexander Pushkin. Pushkin wrote *Boris Godunov*, a play in blank verse based on a real historical character. The play, influenced by Shakespeare's history plays, was an excellent historical drama, but was banned by the censor and was not performed until long after Pushkin's death. Pushkin's short verse dramas are known as the four

Little Tragedies, namely, *Mozart and Salieri*, which was the source for the film *Amadeus; The Stone Guest*, based on the Don Juan theme; *The Covetous Knight*; and *The Feast during the Plague*. Nikolai Gogol, author of the novel *Dead Souls*, also wrote plays, the most famous of which is *The Inspector General*, perhaps the finest of all Russian comedies. The play tells the story of a visitor to a small town who is mistaken for the dreaded inspector general and is treated royally. After the visitor's departure, the townspeople discover their error and, upon the arrival of the real inspector, stand thunderstruck in a moment of silence that marks the end of the play. Ivan Turgenev, author of the novel *Fathers and Sons*, wrote the play *A Month in the Country*, a play about two women after the same man. It is a sensitive study that anticipates the work of Anton Chekhov. Leo Tolstoy, author of *War and Peace*, wrote several plays, among them the harrowing *The Power of Darkness*, a peasant tragedy. A. K. Tolstoy, a distant relative, wrote a trilogy of plays based on Russian history. All these plays are still frequently performed on the Russian stage and are considered classics of the theater.

One of the most prolific playwrights of the nineteenth century was Alexander Ostrovsky, whose plays are still enormously popular in Russia today. Ostrovsky wrote nearly fifty plays; his masterpiece is *The Storm*, the story of a young wife Katerina who is driven to suicide. This work, as is typical of Ostrovsky's plays, is set among the merchant class and features a strong tyrannical character, in this case Katerina's evil mother-in-law. Audiences are particularly fond of his comedy *Poverty Is No Crime*, about a girl whose father intends to marry her off to a rich man instead of the poor man she loves.

Anton Chekhov, the greatest of all Russian playwrights, had a profound impact not just on Russian drama but on world drama. His plays are still performed regularly all over the world. His fame rests mostly on his full-length plays, but one of his most beloved plays is an early short comedy *The Bear*, sometimes also called in English *The Boor*. In this play, a man tries to collect a debt from a young widow. They argue and in a hilarious scene nearly fight a duel, but in the end of course they fall in love.

Chekhov wrote four major full-length plays, *The Seagull* (1896), *Uncle Vanya* (1897), *Three Sisters* (1901), and *The Cherry Orchard* (1904). These plays helped form the basis of modern theater. They have no really exciting action, but are instead a slice of life. As in real life, there is no main character, just a group of characters living out their vaguely frustrating lives, talking past one another without making any real connections. In *Uncle Vanya*, for instance, Vanya and his niece Sonya have skimped and saved to provide money for Sonya's father, a famous professor, and his beautiful new wife Elena, who live in town. When they visit, Vanya discovers that the professor is not worthy of his respect. He and his friend Dr. Astrov, whom plain Sonya secretly loves, both fall in love with Elena. Elena and her husband leave, and life goes on. In *Three Sisters*, each finds her hopes for a better future dashed in different ways.

In Chekhov's most famous play, *The Cherry Orchard*, an aristocratic family ineffectually tries to save their home with its old cherry orchard from being sold to a developer, whose ancestors were serfs on the estate. They are unsuccessful, and the cherry orchard, a symbol of their past, is chopped down. *The Cherry Orchard* is usually thought of as a sad play, a bittersweet farewell to the old, aristocratic Russia of the nineteenth century. This is the way it was staged by Konstantin Stanislavsky, the director who, together with Chekhov, was revolutionizing world theater with his insistence on realism, lack of dramatic action and artificial speech-making, and his abandonment of the star system in favor of an ensemble of actors who shared the limelight equally. Chekhov, who as the grandson of a serf held no great nostalgic affection for the nobility, insisted to Stanislavsky that the play was a comedy. But the play was performed as Stanislavsky wanted it and is still usually performed that way today.

In 1897, Stanislavsky and V. I. Nemirovich-Danchenko founded the Moscow Art Theater, which they envisioned as a public theater that would stage primarily contemporary drama. Chekhov's work was perfect for their theater, which to this day uses a seagull as its symbol. Their ideas for theater extended beyond realism and natural ensemble acting to include creating a unity of impression by paying attention to sets and even the programs. The role of director in interpreting the meaning of a play gained increased importance because of the innovations at the Moscow Art Theater. The stage designer also gained stature.

Another playwright frequently presented at the Moscow Art Theater was Maxim Gorky, author of the very successful *The Lower Depths*, set among derelicts in a flophouse. Before World War I, the Moscow Art Theater moved from the realism of Chekhov to the revolutionary romanticism of Gorky, and then to symbolism.

The revolution coincided with new experiments in theater. Among the great new directors were Evgeny Vakhtangov, Alexander Tairov, and the greatest of all, Vsevolod Meyerhold. Meyerhold reinterpreted plays, staging even the classics in new creative ways, with unusual modern "constructivist" sets, outlandish costumes, and a new method of acting he called biomechanics.

Two outstanding playwrights from this period were Vladimir Mayakovsky and Mikhail Bulgakov. Mayakovsky's best play, staged by Meyerhold, was

The Bedbug, about a man who seems to perish in a fire at his wedding, only to be found and revived, along with a bedbug, far in the future. The audience at first finds him cheap and tasteless, but gains sympathy with him as he is put on exhibit in the sterile, colorless future. Bulgakov, perhaps the best Russian playwright of the twentieth century, wrote several plays, among them the enormously successful *Days of the Turbins*, which incurred the wrath of the communist government because of its sympathetic portrayal of the Whites, the noncommunists, at the time of the revolution.

Although there were some worthy plays written and produced in the succeeding decades, the theater did not again shine as it had in the days of the classic writers or of the great directors Stanislavsky and Meyerhold. Stalin's harsh treatment of experimentation, which resulted in the arrest and execution of Meyerhold, among others; the stiff censorship; and the general lack of freedom made it difficult for Russians to stay in the vanguard of world drama.

With the downfall of communism, Russians were free to create once again. There are many other forms of entertainment competing for attention today, not just the movies and zoos and circuses, but television and video games. Many Russians have little spare money for the theater. Theater is not flourishing, but there are still many plays on stage at any given time in larger cities, as well as productions by theater companies in smaller towns. The Moscow Art Theater, or MKhAT, has a repertoire of some thirty-five plays, and recently featured Tennessee Williams and Molière, as well as Pushkin's *Little Tragedies* and Sergey Dovlatov's *New American*. MKhAT is still known for Stanislavsky's method acting and although it is no longer considered on the cutting edge of theater, it is the best-known drama theater in Russia. Two of the many other fine theaters in Moscow are the Maly and the Sovremennik (Contemporary). Among regional theaters, the one in Magnitogorsk grew to be very successful under the direction of Valery Akhadov.

One popular long-running play is Yuri Lyubimov's production of Bulgakov's novel *The Master and Margarita*, which has had more than a twenty-year run. Bulgakov's *Heart of a Dog* has also enjoyed great success under the direction of Genrietta Yanovskaya, who in 1998 received an award for her new production of Ostrovsky's *The Storm*. The recent period has witnessed the revival of many long-suppressed plays, victims of communist censorship, adding richness to the recent theatrical world as Russians discovered their lost heritage. There have been many talented new playwrights, as well. Playwrights of the most recent period, since 1980, include Alexey Arbuzov, Alexander Gelman, Mikhail Roshchin, Edvard Radzinsky, Nina Sadur, Ludmila Razumovskaya, and Ludmila Petrushevskaya. Petrushevskaya is noted in particular for her portrayal of how ordinary women struggle to live in the lower levels of society, while Sadur mixes mysticism into her unusual plays. Among outstanding recent directors is Roman Vityuk, who has staged Petrushevskaya's work and also a production based on Vladimir Nabokov's *Lolita*.

Puppet theater is much more popular in Russia than in the United States. Several cities have theaters devoted entirely to puppets. The puppets are beautifully made, and careful attention is paid to set construction and music. Puppet shows are usually designed with children in mind, although adults enjoy them also. One prominent puppet theater, the Fairy Tale Theater, has recently mounted such productions as *Aladdin*, Stravinsky's *Petrushka*, Ershov's *The Humpback Horse, Bluebeard, The Ugly Duckling*, and Beaumarchais's comedy *The Barber of Seville*.

Russia awards prizes for excellence in theater. One new award, given only since 1994, is the Gold Mask, which gives awards not only for theater, but for ballet, opera, musicals, and puppet theater. Another prize, the Kumir, or Idol, is given for movie, television, and stage acting. The Stanislavsky Prize goes not only to actors, but to people involved in all aspects of theater work, including directors, composers, and critics, among others.

SUGGESTED READINGS

Brown, David, Gerald Abraham, and David Lloyd-Jones. *Russian Masters I: Glinka, Borodin, Balakirev, Musorgsky, Tchaikovsky*. New York: W. W. Norton, 1986.

Cushman, Thomas. *Notes from Underground: Rock Music Counterculture in Russia*. Albany: State University of New York Press, 1995.

Reeder, Roberta, ed. *Russian Folk Lyrics*. Bloomington: Indiana University Press, 1993.

Russian Life Magazine 2/97, 2/98, 8–9/98, 12/98–1/99, 1–2/00 for popular music.

Zolotov, Andrei, Alexander Gusev, and Yelena Zonina. *The Bolshoi Theatre*. Moscow: Planeta, 1987.

9

Art

ICONS

RUSSIAN ART is not as well known outside Russia as its literature and music. Although there are some excellent painters in the nineteenth and twentieth centuries, the high point of Russian art actually occurred hundreds of years earlier during the golden age of icon painting. The word icon derives from a Greek word meaning image. An icon is a religious picture of Mary, Christ, or a saint, usually painted in tempera on wood. The idea of painting icons came to Russia from Byzantium, along with the Orthodox Christian religion. When Russia became Christian in 988, the Orthodox Church had emerged only a century and a half earlier from a long struggle between the iconoclasts, who wanted to destroy as idolatrous any religious art that represented human or divine figures, and the ultimately victorious iconodules, who thought that the icons could be venerated in the same way as other Christian symbols like the cross. Icon-making took root in Russia, and icons became one of the most familiar features of Russian life.

It is not easy to make an icon in the traditional fashion. Sometimes an icon artist refers to a manual on how to paint an icon for guidance. First, the artist must fast and pray to enter the right spiritual state to create an icon. Only when the artist has achieved the proper frame of mind does the actual work begin. The icon may be painted on a single piece of wood, or on a panel made by joining several pieces together with wooden pins. The wood is cut and smoothed with an ax or sometimes with a plane. Slats behind may prevent warping. A depression may be hollowed out leaving a shallow border.

Perhaps canvas is set in the hollow. A mixture of chalk or alabaster with natural animal glue is applied and dried and smoothed. Then the general design is made and the painting begins. The tempera paint is made primarily of egg yolk and colors derived from natural plant or mineral sources. The icon may also be embellished with gold leaf or paint. After the paint dries, the icon is varnished and polished.

The artist must be careful in choosing the subject matter and style for the icon. Traditional subjects and styles are best. Innovation is not prized because the artist is not showing off his talent but creating an avenue to reveal God and the spirit of the church to the faithful and to carry on tradition from one generation to the next. The figure in the icon does not look like a photograph because the artist is not trying to do a portrait that is true to the physical, earthly appearance but instead is expressing the transfigured perfected image of the subject. The picture looks flat, because there should be no hint this might be a statue, a graven image. The lips and nose tend to be thin, while the eyes, the windows into the soul, are quite large.

The icon may show a close-up, the head and shoulders of a single figure, or a full-length picture. There may be more than one figure or even an entire scene with several figures and trees and smaller plants and buildings or animals. Sometimes several scenes appear on the same icon, perhaps events from the life of a saint, either arranged around the central figure on the icon or arranged in some other design. Sometimes words are written on the icon, often in standard abbreviations, similar to the way people write Xmas for Christmas. Abbreviations are indicated by little wavy marks over the words. It is traditional to write in Old Church Slavonic, a language similar to Russian used in the church. Compared with icons from other areas, Russian icons are distinctive in their large size, their use of brilliant color, their incorporation of elements from the natural world, and their tendency to tell a connected narrative. Different areas of Russia, such as Novgorod, developed distinctive styles.

Icons sometimes had special ornate covers made for them out of precious metals and encrusted with pearls and precious jewels. Sometimes the cover would be enameled. The cover would leave only bits of the icon, such as the hands and face, uncovered.

Icons were everywhere. As might be expected, many belonged to churches. A special screen called the iconostasis divided the public area from the sanctuary in the church. The iconostasis was covered with icons, and icons also appeared elsewhere in the church. Upon entering the church, people would buy a candle, then approach an icon, cross themselves, kiss the icon, and light the candle. People also had icons at home, which were passed down through families but could also be easily acquired at markets. Entering a room, one would see an icon in the "beautiful corner" opposite the door. The icon might stand on a little shelf, illuminated by a small oil lamp. Icons could be placed in barns or stables as well. Icons were even placed at crossroads. People prayed before icons at home and took oaths before them. They brought icons to visit the sick. Icons were carried in all kinds of processions, such as funerals or preparations for battle. Icons could perform miracles and were known to have saved Russia from the enemy on numerous occasions when carried with the army.

Before the 1917 revolution, icons were much more in evidence than they were during the communist era when officially they were admired as art from a past epoch rather than as personally meaningful religious symbols. As communism began to decline in the 1980s, icons began to reappear, in homes and elsewhere. A bus driver might display an icon over the front window of his bus, along with other items that were significant to him, such as pictures of a beautiful model in American jeans and a sleek Italian sports car.

The most venerated of all icons is the Virgin of Vladimir. Legend has it that the Virgin Mary herself posed for the icon, which Luke is said to have painted. The icon actually dates from the twelfth century and was probably brought from Byzantium. It is a picture of Mary with the Christ child and stresses Mary's sad, tender, motherly aspect, which is more important to Russians than her aspect as virgin. The icon has resided in Kiev, then Vladimir, then Moscow, both in a Kremlin church and in the twentieth century in a museum. The icon has saved Russia on more than one occasion and is the most beloved of all icons.

Four icon painters deserve special mention. Feofan Grek (Theophanes the Greek), Andrey Rublev, Dionysius, and Simon Ushakov all painted between the fourteenth and seventeenth centuries. Feofan Grek's work is found in Novgorod and Moscow, where he influenced Andrey Rublev. Dionysius is known for his delicate, mystical icons. Ushakov was the last of the great icon painters. The greatest of the four was undoubtedly Andrey Rublev, who worked in Moscow and Vladimir around 1400 and created the most artistically perfect icon, the Trinity, for Sergey of Radonezh at the monastery at Sergiev Posad. The icon, painted in the colors of the open fields and sky, gold and brown and blue, shows three angels who appeared to Abraham as harbingers of the Father, Son, and Holy Ghost. This icon and the Virgin of Vladimir served as models and inspiration for many later icons.

Numerous icons show the Virgin and Child or scenes from the life of Christ. Some of the other saints depicted in icons are quite familiar to Westerners, but not all. Attributes of the old thunder god were transferred to

Elijah, who brings rain to the good and fire or hail to the bad. He is often pictured being carried to heaven in a chariot. St. George, protector of cattle, peasants, prisoners, and warriors, is shown on a white horse against a red background, slaying a dragon. St. Nicholas, the patron saint of Russia, protects sailors and fishermen, children and travelers. St. Paraskeva or Pyatnitsa (Friday) wears the red of a martyr, and is the patron of women's domestic work. She might prick the finger of someone who sews on her day, Friday. The martyrs Boris and Gleb, the first Russian saints, are pictured together. St. Nicetas is pictured beating the devil.

Under communism, some icons were transferred to museums, while many others were destroyed. Icon painters found other work, some of them turning to folk crafts. Today in Russia icon painters are once again creating their beautiful images of Christ, Mary, and the saints. Some icons have been moved from museums back to churches. Although icons do not occupy the place in Russian life that they once did, they are still an important part of the Russian cultural landscape.

PAINTING AND OTHER ART

Russian painters of the nineteenth century are not considered of the same caliber and are not as well known outside Russia as the writers and musicians of the same period. Part of the reason for that has been the tendency to study Western art of the period as the triumph of the reaction of modernist movements like French Impressionism over the academic tradition. Russian artists of that same period also rebelled, but their rebellion was in a different direction. Rather than being interested in exploring the play of form and color, they wanted to produce art with social content that had some relevance to reforming Russian life. Their movement became known as the Itinerants or Wanderers because of their intention to take their paintings out to the people by means of traveling exhibitions.

The Itinerants were not the first or only significant nineteenth-century Russian painters. The most celebrated painter before the Itinerants was Karl Bryullov, who came to Russia from Italy as a child. His early fame rested on a painting of the destruction of Pompeii, but today it is his rich, lush portraits of his contemporaries that attract the viewer. Another noteworthy artist was Alexander Ivanov, who spent two decades working on a painting of Christ's appearance before the people. Foreshadowing the social conscience of the Itinerants, Pavel Fedotov painted scenes from contemporary life like *The Major's Courtship*, in which a young merchant's daughter is obviously resisting attempts to marry her off to a self-satisfied man who stands just outside the doorway, confidently twirling his mustache. Alexey Venetsianov also helped pave the way for the Itinerants with his scenes of peasant life.

The students at the Academy of Art rebelled in 1863, reluctant to compete for a prize for painting a scene showing the mythical Valhalla. They formed their own group, the Itinerants, who would work as a community of artists, sharing rather than competing with one another. They would paint subjects relevant to the great social ferment in Russia rather than waste time on subjects of no benefit to the Russian people. They interpreted this idea broadly, including subjects like Christ, whose suffering humanity seemed as apt a subject as a picture of contemporary society. They were right in tune with their times, a period when Turgenev wrote his great social novel *Fathers and Sons* and all of intellectual Russia was engrossed in the subject of reform. The leader of the Itinerants was Ivan Kramskoy, known for his fine portraits and for his depiction of *Christ in the Wilderness*.

The leading Itinerant artist was Ilya Repin (1844–1930), the best known of all Russian artists of the period. His painting *Volga Boatmen*, with its depiction of downtrodden men hauling a heavy barge down the great river, offered a ray of hope as one young hauler in the picture looks into the distance toward a better future. In addition to works on contemporary life, Repin painted a number of historical scenes, most notably his picture of Ivan the Terrible with the son he has just murdered. The painting was very controversial and was even banned for a time, because it reminded people that this murder broke the direct line of descent in the royal family, calling into question the authority of the Romanov dynasty. Among Repin's many other excellent paintings is one of a religious procession in Kursk, contrasting the insensitive representatives of the powerful church and state with the suffering villagers.

The Itinerant movement continued to dominate the rest of the century and the early twentieth century. Among the many other Itinerant painters toward the end of the century are Vasily Surikov, known for his historical scenes, and Isaak Levitan, one of the finest Russian landscape artists. Not all paintings were done by artists associated with the Itinerants. The huge gorgeous seascapes by Ivan Ayvazovsky, for example, lie outside the Itinerant movement.

A hint at a new kind of art came with the work of Mikhail Vrubel, who was not interested in painting Christ or broad Russian landscapes or scenes with social content. Nor did he favor the Itinerants' smooth flat realism, with barely a visible brushstroke to draw the eye. Vrubel experimented with color, paint texture, and form, and his subject matter included many variations of the Demon or devil. He and other artists of the time were more concerned with art for art's sake than with art for social improvement.

At the turn of the century, designers who would become known in the West, like Leon Bakst and Alexander Benois, and other artists and illustrators, like the fairy-tale illustrator Ivan Bilibin, were members of a group that formed around the journal *Mir Iskusstva*, or *World of Art*. This journal was succeeded by others as Russians spent the early part of the twentieth century becoming better acquainted both with world art and with their own folk-art heritage, which would eventually result in an explosion of creativity, producing avant-garde art of the first rank, some of the best work done anywhere in the early twentieth century.

Two of the main figures in the development of this new art were Natalya Goncharova and her companion, Mikhail Larionov. To distance themselves from earlier groups that they considered too interested in the ethereal and in the symbolic, the new artists chose down-to-earth names like Donkey's Tail for their group exhibits. They experimented with primitivism and new techniques with names like "rayonnism." The artists adopted such terms as Cubo-Futurism for their work. A Goncharova painting might show peasants dancing, with large, flat, blocklike figures. Or she might paint a man on a bicycle with rhythmic lines, indicating movement while bits of words floated about the picture. The works had recognizable subjects but were rendered in a radically new, modern way. Kazimir Malevich also experimented with primitivism, then abandoned identifiable subjects temporarily in favor of pure abstraction, going so far as to paint a white square tilted against a white background, or perhaps just a black square. At this time there were a number of female artists besides Goncharova in the front ranks of experimental art, among them Lyubov Popova, an abstract artist, and Alexandra Exter, who, in addition to painting, also designed the costumes for the futuristic film *Aelita Queen of Mars* in the 1920s.

The two painters from this period that are most familiar to Americans are Wassily Kandinsky and Marc Chagall. Kandinsky is considered the first artist to have painted a completely abstract work of art. Chagall, who was born in the Belarussian town Vitebsk, used images from his hometown to create fanciful pictures that were a forerunner of surrealism. Both artists left Russia in the early 1920s and continued working in the West for the rest of their lives.

In the early 1920s, a new movement in Russia, Constructivism, reflected the interest of the new society in industry and science. Artists used such materials as metal or glass to build objects like Vladimir Tatlin's *Monument to the Third International*, a model for a huge tower with levels rotating at different speeds. Other artists devoted themselves to making posters or designing fabrics for the new society, and still others engaged in realistic paintings depicting the life of workers, peasants, and political figures.

The rich diversity of the 1920s gave way to repression in the following decades, as the government began to exert more control over the types of art that met its approval. The communist regime wanted art that promoted communism and art that was easily understood by the common person. The communist doctrine of Socialist Realism allowed no room for artists who wanted to indulge in abstract art or in any form of art that was deemed too concerned with "formal" considerations rather than content. Portraits of communist leaders like Lenin and Stalin met with approval, as did Vera Mukhina's large metal statue of a male factory worker and female farm worker, holding aloft a hammer and a sickle, symbols of the new society. The great flowering of modern art in the first decades of the century withered. Until the thaw after the death of Stalin in 1953, mainstream Russian art was cut off from the modernism that continued to develop in the West. Some good realistic paintings were done, but nothing that would be considered of the caliber of the previous generation. In the area of photography, Evgeny Khaldei did some remarkable work, including his famous photograph of raising the Soviet flag over Berlin in 1945.

After 1956, there was some effort to reconnect with the experimental work of the earlier part of the century and also with art being created outside Russia, but realistic art continued to dominate the art scene, especially since the government cracked down on artists who strayed too far from the approved norm. They might be ignored, deprived of commissions, or in extreme cases even beaten or sent to camps or to psychiatric hospitals. In 1974, a group of artists incurred the wrath of the authorities by mounting a large, unofficial outdoor display of their art. The authorities attracted world attention when, armed with bulldozers and fire hoses, they smashed and burned their way through the exhibit. Artists continued to press for freedom of expression, and the government responded by easing up slightly on unofficial art while at the same time allowing, or even forcing, some artists to emigrate.

At the end of the 1980s as the Soviet Union began to collapse, there were many kinds of artists: artists pursuing traditional official art, those working within official art who used elements of Impressionist technique to paint scenes from nature, those seeking to recapture the artistic Russian past of icons or of the great artists earlier in the twentieth century, and those engaging in experimental art or following Western trends. Some were working in other mediums, such as photography, for example, Vladimir Syomin, who recorded unusual scenes of everyday life in Russia.

Under communism, many Russian artists were trained at government-supervised art academies, where, after years of rigorous training, they might be invited to join the official union of artists. The government offered commissions for art projects and provided support for artists and also organized competitions and exhibitions. Artists did not have to worry much about marketing themselves or their works. Artists working in nonapproved styles did not enjoy such support, and had to rely on other means, such as a day job or a spouse, to keep food on the table.

When communism fell, conditions suddenly changed for all the artists. Exhibits of once-forbidden art were very popular. Artists could paint without fear of official reprisals and could openly exhibit and market their works. They could travel outside the country. On the other hand, there were new worries. There were not as many government commissions or other handouts. Artists had to learn how to market their art, deal with galleries, collectors, and auction houses, and figure out how to get financial support from new sources, such as foreign buyers or businesses.

Aside from financial considerations, the artists were not in agreement about what kind of art to make or even whether art mattered in the new Russia. Artists noted that there was interest in looking at exhibits of banned work for a while, but that soon the public ignored art and seemed more interested in popular culture and in just living from day to day in the uncertain economy. As might be expected, the conservative Union of Artists still favored those who worked in the realist tradition. Some artists wanted to join the West and create art in the current Western modes, while others wanted to absorb modern foreign culture and from that create a new kind of Russian art. Still others deplored Western modern art, as well as the culturally barren life in modern Russia, and wanted to return to the past, to classical art or Orthodox art, for inspiration.

The art establishment still favored painting above any other kind of art, but in the 1990s, artists were busily engaged in other forms of art. Photography engaged some artists. One artist, Denis Sidorov, attached copies of photos of victims of the conflict in Chechnya to meat-can lids to stress the fact that they were cannon fodder. Still others were making videos. Alexander Roitburd combined cuts from the famous Odessa Steps scene in the Eisenstein movie *Battleship Potemkin* with scenes of rollerblading and clips from an American movie to create a new "psychedelic" work of art, as the artist termed it. Computer collages and even Internet art, such as that designed by

Olya Lyalina to be flashed from server to server around the world, began to appear. Some artists made installations, while others engaged in performance art, like Natalya Pershina and Olga Egorova, who jumped off a bridge into water in "Poor Liza," after the Karamzin story of that name, where the heroine commits suicide by drowning.

Around the actual works of art swirl such terms as Freudianism, semiotics, the Russian Cézannes, the Penza school, Neo-Academism, and many others. Modern Russian art had its roots in Pop Art and in so-called Sots-Art, a kind of combination of Pop-Art and Socialist Realism, out of which came Conceptualism, where the idea of the art object was more important than the art itself. An example was Ilya Kabakov's work *Man of Rubbish*, trash attached to a stand and carefully labeled.

Like many other artists, Kabakov moved to the West, where he continued working and exhibiting. Artists outside the conservative mainstream, who remained in Russia, exhibited in galleries hospitable to them or even in apartments. As late as 1998, the official union galleries were still not exhibiting video or computer art. Few museums were actively pursuing a policy of collecting a wide variety of contemporary art or even had a representative collection of the various kinds of art since the thaw after Stalin's death. One of the best collections of underground, unofficial art of the period 1956–1986 was in the United States at Rutgers, containing thousands of pieces collected by American scholar Norton Dodge on his trips to Russia. The finest collections of Russian art from earlier periods are to be found at the Tretyakov Gallery in Moscow and at the Russian Museum in St. Petersburg. The collection in the Russian Museum is larger, but the finest pieces are to be found in the Tretyakov. Since the fall of communism, museums have struggled to get enough funding to carry out their mission. With state funding in peril, they have sought corporate sponsors with some success.

The best-known museum in Russia is the Hermitage in St. Petersburg. The Hermitage is a repository of world art, one of the finest museums in the world. Its collection of French Impressionist paintings is legendary. Its counterpart in Moscow is the Pushkin Museum.

FOLK ART AND DECORATIVE ART

With so much land covered by forest and so much time spent indoors during the long cold winters, it is no wonder that Russians long ago became adept at folk arts made of wood. Besides creating elaborately carved and painted window frames and other external ornamentation, Russians made festively decorated wooden furniture and other household implements such as distaffs, used in needlework, and spoons, bowls, and boxes. Sometimes the wood is intricately carved, almost lacy, with flowers, geometric figures, and animals, and then left unpainted. Or it may be partly or entirely covered with paint. Sometimes the item is not carved but is still decorated with painted flowers or horses or birds, usually with the background left in the natural pale wood color. Certain areas of Russia became known for the style of their work. Work from Gorodets, for example, often features brightly painted horses and flowers on an unpainted background of uncarved wood.

The villages near the trading center Khokhloma developed a process for treating their painted wooden bowls, trays, spoons, and other wooden items that is highly distinctive and immediately recognizable, perhaps the best-known regional type. After a process of sealing the surface of the object with clay and then coating it with linseed oil and drying it in an oven, the object is ready to be painted. Powdered metal such as tin, or more recently aluminum, and paints, usually black and red with a touch of green, are applied, with either the black or the metal as the background color, depicting leaves, vines, flowers, and berries. When the object is then varnished and put back in the oven, the powdered metal takes on a gold sheen and the whole object glows. Khokhloma ware is durable but seems almost too beautiful to use to serve food, as is sometimes done.

For hundreds of years Russians have also made toys out of wood, especially aspen, alder, maple, and linden, soft woods that are easier to carve. Today, like other wooden items, they are made both professionally and by private individuals, who may create them as art, for amusement, or for profit. The toys often represent people or animals and sometimes can perform tricks if the toy is manipulated in a certain way. For instance, birds might bob their heads as if pecking at grain if a little peg is pushed in and out of the base on which they are mounted. In another toy, strings attached to a ball make a little wooden woman's arms go up and down as if she is sewing when a child whirls the ball around. Often the toys are left unpainted, or have only a touch of paint with some of the bare wood left showing.

One wooden toy developed in the late nineteenth century in the area of Sergiev Posad has become very popular both as a toy and as an art object. This is the *matryoshka*, or nesting doll. The word is a diminutive, or nickname, for Matryona, a name widely used among the Russian people at that time. The outermost doll is gently curved with a flat base and pulls apart around the middle to reveal a slightly smaller doll within. That doll also comes apart, revealing yet another doll. A simple matryoshka might have only three or four dolls, while a more elaborate one might have two dozen or even five dozen, nested one within the other. The innermost doll is usually quite small, and does not come apart. Usually the dolls are painted identically, although some sets feature all different dolls. Typically a stylized young woman in peasant dress decorated with a flower motif is depicted. In the last decade, artists have been making fancier dolls, signing them and selling them as art objects. Most still show young women, but there are also matryoshkas of other types. One popular kind, widely imitated, shows Yeltsin, with figures of Gorbachev, Brezhnev, Stalin, and Lenin inside. One beautiful set shows such literary figures as Pushkin and Tolstoy, with scenes from their literary works depicted on the back. Some sets today even feature Disney characters, or American political figures, or scenes from famous paintings, or tsars.

Russians have also engaged in metal work. The metal deposits in the Ural Mountains served as a resource for metalworkers who created various types of household implements such as tableware or goblets, often decorated with birds or vines. A hundred years ago, the iron workers of Kasli were renowned for their intricate statues and decorative pieces of cast iron. Niello work, adapted from Western European practices, has been a Russian specialty for centuries and is still made today. Niello work involves engraving a design on a piece of silver and filling the grooves with a mixture composed primarily of powdered metal, which fuses and blackens when exposed to heat. The black tracery creates a beautiful pattern on the silver, which can be as simple as a design of flowers, or as complex as a whole scene from the city or countryside. Artisans in the Urals also have recently been making ceremonial metal swords. In the village of Zhostovo near Moscow, artisans have been painting and lacquering metal trays for two hundred years. The trays typically are black, less often red, green, or blue, with a delicate gold border of flowers or leaves. In the center are bouquets of colorful flowers, such as roses, or occasionally a selection of fruits or birds instead of flowers.

Russia is also known for its items made of clay. For centuries people around the village of Dymkovo have made clay objects. At first these objects may have been associated with seasonal festivals, although later they were thought of simply as toys or collectibles. The objects, which range in size from an inch to 4 inches, are made by women, sometimes assisted by children. The clay is shaped, and if the figure has more than one part, the parts are joined together, and then the figure is dried and fired. The figures are then coated in a chalky mixture, which provides a white background for the paint that is applied next. The women apply anywhere from four to more than a dozen colors and may use a bit of gold as well. At first figures were usually animals such as sheep, cows, pigs, horses, or chickens, as well as more fantastic creatures. Later human figures became popular, and often were made to be displayed in groups engaged in some village activity. Today Dymkovo figures are widely admired and are sold far beyond the village of Dymkovo. In the 1990s young people often made imitations of famous crafts like Dymkovo to sell to tourists. Because this is a woman's craft, it was natural for a group of teenage girls to try their hand at making little clay animals to supplement the family income. In a related genre, the artist Irina Emelina has developed her own type of ceramics and has gained recognition for her figurines, which are grouped together in scenes like a marketplace or bathhouse.

Gzhel pottery is also quite famous. Artisans have been making pottery in the Gzhel area not far from Moscow since the 1600s. They soon began specializing in majolica and later also made faience and porcelain. The most common type of Gzhel ware today is white with dark blue designs, similar to Dutch Delft ware, although some Gzhel is made in other colors. Gzhel artisans make fanciful covered dishes, candlestick holders, vases, tea sets, jars, and animal figurines. A typical piece might be a deep dish decorated with flowers, with a lid with a three-dimensional cow or chicken perched on top. Mention should also be made of the Lomonosov porcelain factory in St. Petersburg, where some of Russia's finest china is made.

Perhaps the most beautiful craft made in Russia is the handpainted box. Four areas specialize in these boxes, each with its own style of painting: Palekh, Fedoskino, Kholui, and Mstera. Fedoskino made thousands of hand-made lacquer boxes in the nineteenth century. After the 1917 revolution, icon painters in Palekh turned to making boxes as well, soon followed by icon makers in Kholui and Mstera. The process of making a traditional papier-mâché box is quite time-consuming, involving cutting, gluing, and pressing cardboard onto a form, drying it, boiling it in oil, applying several coats of base and lacquer, and various other steps, taking perhaps two months to produce a very strong box, usually painted black outside, and red inside. The artist paints a very detailed, beautiful scene on the box, often using a magnifying glass and special brushes, and finishes off the design by applying touches of gold trim. The box may be polished smooth with a wolf's tooth. Palekh artists may use egg-based tempera paint. Their boxes, which many consider the most beautiful of all, often feature scenes, even multiple scenes, from fairy tales or literature, with elongated willowy figures and fanciful plants. Kholui boxes feature more substantial, realistic figures, with more of an all-over design, as do Mstera boxes, which tend to have pale backgrounds. Fedoskino boxes, like the others, use fairy tale scenes, but also copy famous paintings and show village scenes, again using more substantial figures than Palekh boxes. Fedoskino boxes often use metallic undercoating covered with thin oil painting and seem luminous as a result. Under communism, box makers sometimes showed scenes from contemporary life. Today rich New

Russians have been known to commission boxes showing scenes from their own opulent lifestyle.

In Kholmogory in the Russian North, the inhabitants have long carved graceful translucent figurines of animals and humans out of yellowish whale tooth and out of white bone, both very hard substances. Today they also make such decorative items as paper knives, brooches, and boxes. In Tobolsk, in Siberia, Russians also carve bone, creating reindeer or a dog team pulling a sleigh, scenes from contemporary life. Bone carving is also done in the far eastern regions of Russia.

Birch bark, or *beresta*, is another natural element used in art. The bark is soft and easily woven and has long been used to make baskets and shoes. It has also been used to a limited extent in recent years to produce decorated items for the home, such as containers for bread, butter, or even milk.

Women's needlework is treated in the chapter on costume, but mention should be made here of the household items and items for the church made by women. Embroidered towels, draped around icons, were particularly beautiful. For the church, women made sewn icons. Women began making sewn icons many hundreds of years ago. They used luxurious materials and metallic thread to create icons that were as precious and honored as the painted ones from which many of them were copied. The art of sewn icons was almost lost during the communist era, but is enjoying a modest revival today.

Needlework fell outside the narrow bounds of officially recognized art under communism, which meant that it was not considered particularly useful for propaganda purposes. This gave fiber artists a measure of freedom to experiment with form and design, using quilting, batik, weaving, embroidery, painting, and other techniques to create work that rivals similar fabric work in the West during the same period. The work of Ludmila Uspenskaya is an example of this type of craft.

Russian crafts have traditionally been highly prized, both in Russia and in the West. Some villages that specialized in certain crafts found their work institutionalized after the 1917 revolution, with factories developed to continue the work, sometimes with a decline in quality. Today once again private individuals and groups are recovering their heritage and beginning to produce excellent work.

Not all crafts and decorative work were done in villages. The most famous decorative craft pieces of late tsarist times were the work of Faberge, a firm that specialized in exquisite handcrafted individual items for moneyed clients, such as cigarette cases and miniature animal figures made of precious stones and metals and often enameled. The best-known pieces were the Easter eggs made for the tsar's family. The two artists most closely involved were Mikhail

Perchin, who made the earlier eggs, and Henrik Wigstrom, his foreign assistant who succeeded him. An example is Perchin's Resurrection egg, a rock crystal egg containing figures of Christ and angels mounted on a stand decorated with enamel, pearls, and diamonds. It stands nearly 4 inches tall. Some eggs contain a surprise. Perchin's golden-yellow diamond-encrusted Coronation egg contains a miniature of the coronation coach, correct in every detail, and his pink Lilies-of-the-Valley egg contains portraits of the tsar and his two daughters. Carl Faberge, the firm's head, closed up shop and left Russia at the time of the revolution, but his firm's work is still admired and imitated today. Some of the more than fifty eggs have been lost, but many of those remaining can be seen in the Kremlin or in various collections in the United States and Europe.

SUGGESTED READINGS

Bird, Alan. *A History of Russian Painting.* Boston: G. K. Hall, 1987.

Gray, Camilla. *The Russian Experiment in Art 1863–1922.* London: Thames and Hudson, 1986.

Hamilton, George Heard. *The Art and Architecture of Russia.* New Haven, CT: Yale University Press, 1983.

Hilton, Alison. *Russian Folk Art.* Bloomington: Indiana University Press, 1995.

McPhee, John. *The Ransom of Russian Art.* New York: Farrar, Straus, Giroux, 1994.

Rice, Tamara Talbot. *A Concise History of Russian Art.* New York: Frederick A. Praeger, 1967.

The Internet at www.moma.org/online projects/internyet is a good source for information on art today.

10

Architecture

HOMES

MUCH OF EARLY RUSSIA was forested, so it was natural for people to build their homes of wood. Villages often grew up beside rivers, with wooden houses lining a road that ran near the river. In southern regions where wood was harder to come by, brick or a whitewashed clay mixture were more common building materials. The house might be raised on stones or tree stumps as a kind of foundation, and roofs were made of wood or thatched. Houses could be of various sizes, even two-storied. Sometimes humans and animals were housed under one roof, especially in the north where it was cold walking from one building to another in winter, or there might be a house with separate outbuildings.

The main room of the village house was dominated by the stove, called the *pech*. The stove was huge, a big block of clay or brick, often whitewashed, with an opening in the side where food could be inserted and a flat surface where people could lie down and stay warm. The stove heated the room and cooked the food and dried the clothes and served as a bed for the old, the very young, or the sick. The smoke from the stove usually was allowed to rise to the ceiling, where a duct carried it out of the house. Such houses were known as black houses, as opposed to white houses that had brick chimneys. Lining the walls were benches, where people might sit or sleep. People might also sleep on a wide shelf that lay atop the stove and stretched across the room. There would also be a table and stools and perhaps a cradle hanging from the ceiling for the baby. In olden times, water might be fetched from a well. Lighting was provided by windows, and, at night, if necessary, by burning torches or sometimes by kerosene.

The houses might be beautified by stitchery made by the women of the house. Especially beautiful would be the corner set aside for the icon shelf, where a piece of embroidered cloth, known as a towel, would be draped around the icon, under which a small flame burned. Some of the furniture might also be decorated with carvings or paint. Outside, the windows were usually surrounded by elaborate carved frames, in endless variations of colors and shapes. Some wooden structures also had carvings on the edge of the roof and on other parts of the exterior. The houses sported carved flowers, leaves, geometric shapes, swirls, birds, lions, and other animals both real and imaginary. One popular figure was the sirin, a birdlike creature with a woman's face and breasts and a feathered tail. Homes of people outside the peasant class might also be decorated with such carvings, which became widely esteemed by connoisseurs of folk crafts in the late nineteenth century.

In the twentieth century, the communist regime was most interested in providing inexpensive housing for large numbers of people. In large cities like Moscow, apartments became the norm, with a small amount of living space allotted for each person. Huge plain blocks of apartments arose; often facilities such as kitchens and bathrooms were shared among several families. When sharing proved unpopular, eventually apartments were constructed with separate facilities, but these new apartments were often smaller and shoddier than older apartments. Today most city-dwellers live in apartments with one or more rooms in addition to their own kitchen and bath. The bathroom is divided into two rooms, one for the tub and sink and another for the toilet. In apartments with only one additional room, that room serves as a living room, dining room, and bedroom. Larger apartments may have a separate bedroom and living room. Outside the biggest cities, in smaller cities and also in the countryside, some houses are available. The houses are frequently wooden. Some may even resemble a log cabin, with logs stacked one above the other to form the outer walls, while most others have a more modern look.

In Russian dwellings, windows are frequently double, one set inside the other, for added insulation. A small special pane in the window called a *fortochka* can be opened for fresh air. Furniture tends to be rather large and dark, or else have a simple Scandinavian look. Russians tend to mix several patterns in a single room more than Americans would, rather than combining one pattern with solid colors. Russians are fond of hanging patterned rugs on the wall for decoration.

Many Russians who live in cities have *dachas*, or houses in the country.

These may be very simple, perhaps without running water or sometimes without electricity. People may go there on weekends or for part of the summer, and many grow gardens to supplement their food supply. At the dacha, they may visit, play sports, walk in the woods, or simply relax. Most dachas are constructed of wood, which is in such abundant supply in Russia.

CHURCHES

Russia has a long tradition of wooden architecture for public buildings, as well as for houses. Unfortunately wood burns easily, and fires were a constant problem in Russia. However, some beautiful wooden churches survived. Some are very small village churches, but there are also some magnificent examples of larger wooden churches. The most famous is the Church of the Transfiguration of the Savior at Kizhi, which is nearly three hundred years old. It stands among other examples of wooden architecture in a field of wild flowers near the shimmering waters of the far north. It towers high above its surroundings, with a profusion of nearly two dozen wooden domes rising in tiers against the sky. Russians cut wood for buildings like these with an ax rather than with a saw, so that the grain of the wood would be smashed together rather than opened up and the wood would be more durable. The building was fitted together without a single nail. Up close, the elegantly carved shingles on the domes can be clearly seen. They are made of aspen, which almost gleams in the sunlight. There are other collections of wooden architecture that have been assembled and preserved in Russia, but none are as impressive as the one at Kizhi.

Some early churches were first built of wood and later replaced with other materials, such as limestone covered with cement. Many of these churches built of more permanent materials still survive. At the same time that the great gray Gothic cathedrals like Notre Dame with their vaulting arches and jewel-like windows were rising in the West, Russia was building quite different churches in the East. Influenced by architecture from Byzantium and from Kiev, churches such as Novgorod's St. Sophia, a very early example from the eleventh century, and the Church of the Intercession on the Nerl, often considered the finest example of medieval Russian architecture, were being constructed. Russian churches tended to be square, with one or more domes rising up toward heaven. The church on the Nerl is a simple white cube, but lovely in its simplicity. Its setting was carefully thought out. It sits alone on an artificial hill gently rising near the meeting of two rivers. Novgorod, Vladimir, Suzdal, and Pskov all have outstanding examples of medieval churches. Sometimes the basic square shape is modified with additions

to one or more sides, and the square shape is softened with pointed or curved roofs over the additions. The sides of the building often have elaborate designs raised onto or sunk into the surface.

The most distinctive feature of Russian churches is their domes. Early Russian domes are helmet-shaped, rather than the familiar bulbous onion shape that came into wide use later. The origin of the onion domes is uncertain, but they have become the most recognizable feature of the Russian building style. Russian domes are often gold or silver, but some of the most beautiful are deep blue with gold stars on them. The tiny city of Suzdal, once a great power, is the home of the lovely Cathedral of the Nativity of the Virgin, shining white against a blue sky, and capped with even deeper blue domes sprinkled with golden six-pointed stars and topped with glistening gold crosses.

The most famous building in Russia, capped with numerous colorful onion domes, is St. Basil's Cathedral on Red Square in Moscow. St. Basil's was built in the sixteenth century by Ivan the Terrible to commemorate the taking of Kazan. More formally known as the Cathedral of the Intercession on the Moat, today it is widely known as St. Basil's. Kazan was taken on the holiday dedicated to the Intercession of the Virgin, while St. Basil, a *yurodivy*, or fool in Christ, highly esteemed by the Russian people and by Ivan the Terrible himself, died in the same year as that great victory. The church, designed by Barma and Postnik Yakovlev, is located on high ground near the Moscow River just outside the walls of Kremlin. The church appears to the casual eye as a colorful profusion of towers and domes with no immediately discernible plan. However, the original plan was quite carefully thought out, though slightly obscured by later additions. The central core of the church is surrounded on the east, west, north, and south by four large eight-sided churches, with four smaller square churches set between them, all eight designed to have separate entrances. Topping the churches are towers with domes, with the central core topped by a tall tower with a pointed tent roof with a tiny dome on top. A much smaller tower with yet another dome is nestled between two larger towers on one side, while on the other side, extensions stretch out left and right, widening the appearance of the church. The original church was much less colorful than it would later become. The original domes, of unknown shape but perhaps of a single color, were replaced by onion domes, or *lukovitsy*, after a fire in the sixteenth century. Much colored ornamentation was added to the outside of the church in the next century. Today the building with its fanciful multicolored domes and richly decorated exterior is breathtaking in its beauty, a reminder not just of the spirituality of the Russian people, but of their exuberance and originality.

The inside of St. Basil's, because it is composed of various small components, is not as impressive as one would expect from outside. Much more beautiful inside is one of the churches nearby, the Cathedral of the Assumption, sometimes called the Cathedral of the Dormition. In Russian it is called the Uspensky Cathedral. This is the largest of the three major churches on Cathedral Square inside the Kremlin. All three were built in the hundred years before St. Basil's. The Assumption Cathedral, designed by an Italian architect, combines features of earlier Russian churches with European structural innovations. The architect's design ensured that the gorgeous colors of the icons and frescoes would be bathed in light, lending magnificence to this vast open room that would be used to crown the Russian rulers. Outside the church seems rather plain when compared with St. Basil's, though it has huge gilded domes. The Cathedral of the Annunciation, or Blagoveshchensky Cathedral, was built by Russian architects on the site of an earlier church, from which were preserved some of Russia's most treasured icons by Feofan Grek and Andrey Rublev. The third cathedral, the Cathedral of the Archangel Michael, or Arkhangelsky Cathedral, was designed by an Italian architect and features large decorative scallops on the exterior. This cathedral houses the tombs of the early Russian tsars; the later ones are in St. Petersburg.

These are only a few of the multitude of Russian-style domed churches dotting the Russian landscape and giving a distinctly Russian look to cities that would never be mistaken for American cities. Moscow was once known for its huge number of churches. Moscow's incomparable Novodevichy convent and its church look like a fairy-tale kingdom from a distance across the Moscow River. In the area near Moscow called the Golden Ring, cities like Kostroma, Yaroslavl, and Rostov, to mention only a few, have excellent examples of church architecture.

Unlike the churches in Moscow and other old cities, most of St. Petersburg's churches are very Western in appearance. Two of the best known date to the early nineteenth century and feature classical columns and a large central dome. St. Isaac's Cathedral is immense, capable of holding thousands of people. It is richly decorated inside with malachite columns. Kazan Cathedral features a semicircular colonnade influenced by St. Peter's in Rome. The church was used by the communists to house a museum of religion and atheism, with displays showing the excesses of religion over the centuries.

The communists took great care of some churches regarded as historical treasures of the Russian people, although they used many of these as museums rather than as houses of worship. The huge nineteenth-century Cathedral of Christ the Savior in Moscow was not so lucky. It was blown up in Stalinist times. Even Red Square was not safe from the wreckers. Although St. Basil's

escaped destruction, another small church on Red Square, the three-hundred-year-old Kazan Cathedral, was demolished, as were the Iberia Chapel and the historic Resurrection Gates, the main entrance to Red Square.

All across Russia, many other churches and religious structures like monasteries are crumbling from seventy years of neglect. Most are of architectural or historical significance or are valued for their sentimental or religious aspect. Work has been done to restore and refurbish some of them, but money is scarce, and many other tasks besides restoring churches face Russians today as they try to build a new society.

OTHER ARCHITECTURE: MOSCOW AND ST. PETERSBURG

At the heart of Moscow on high ground lies the original fortress of the city, the Kremlin. The Kremlin is a triangular shaped plot of land enclosed by a high thick wall. Inside are churches, government buildings, and numerous other structures built over the last several centuries. The original Kremlin was much smaller and was enclosed by a wooden wall. It was later enlarged and surrounded by a new stone wall, which was finally replaced by the present wall of brick. In places, the wall is more than 50 feet high and more than 15 feet thick. Numerous towers rise along the perimeter of the wall.

Inside the Kremlin, many buildings have come and gone, razed to make way for grander structures or torn down for other design schemes. The most beautiful buildings are the churches on Cathedral Square built in the fifteenth and sixteenth centuries. Nearby is another early structure, the white Ivan the Great Belltower, topped by a gilded dome. Like several other Kremlin structures of the time, it was designed by an Italian architect. Beside the Belltower is the Tsar Bell, the heaviest bell in the world, with a large piece chipped out of it. People have their pictures taken by the bell and also by the nearby Tsar Cannon, a 40-ton cannon that has never been fired. Yet another early Italian-designed building is the Palace of Facets with its distinctive faceted limestone walls. Here the tsars had reception rooms and a throne room. Other palaces include the seventeenth-century Terem Palace and the nineteenth-century Great Kremlin Palace. Some rooms in the palaces are elegant in the Western fashion, but more interesting are the opulent Russian rooms, reminiscent of the styles seen in the design of St. Basil's.

Many of the government buildings in the Kremlin are a rich yellow in color, classical in appearance, and were built in the eighteenth and nineteenth centuries. One of the yellow buildings houses the Armory, a museum containing jewels, gold carriages, weaponry, clothing, thrones, and other items

of interest. Particularly beautiful are the fur-rimmed crowns and other regalia of the tsars.

Peter the Great moved the Russian capital to St. Petersburg at the beginning of the eighteenth century, where it remained throughout tsarist times. It is no surprise that some of the finest examples of architecture from that period are in St. Petersburg. Like Washington, St. Petersburg was a planned city. While Moscow seemed to develop in widening circles from its Kremlin core, St. Petersburg has as its heart the Peter-Paul Fortress. St. Petersburg is crisscrossed with arms of the Neva River, as well as with canals, from which comes its name Venice of the North. The main street is the long, straight, wide Nevsky Prospect. Along the waterways and flanking the streets are beautiful pastel buildings, many designed by West European architects in Baroque and Neoclassical styles.

From the earliest period come the Cathedral of Saints Peter and Paul, where the later tsars are buried, and the Kunstkammer, a museum of everyday objects from around the world, as well as oddities from nature. In the next generation, the Italian Bartolomeo Rastrelli did significant work on palaces, such as the Winter Palace, Peterhof, and Tsarskoe Selo, all in the Baroque style. The Winter Palace was later enlarged by additions known as the Hermitage to hold the royal collection of paintings. The Hermitage (in Russian, *Ermitazh*) today is one of the premier art museums in the world. The taking of the Winter Palace in 1917, where the provisional government was meeting in the months after the overthrow of the tsarist government, signaled the beginning of more than seventy years of communist rule. Today painted pale green, the Winter Palace stands serenely on the banks of the Neva, one of the loveliest buildings in Russia. Rastrelli's Peterhof is located outside St. Petersburg near the Gulf of Finland. Standing on high ground, a sweep of golden fountains adds to its beauty. The interior of Peterhof was destroyed by German invaders in World War II, but it has been carefully restored, as have been many of the fountains that decorate the grounds. The Catherine Palace at Tsarskoe Selo, which Empress Elizabeth hoped would rival Versailles, also suffered damage during World War II, but has been restored. Still under reconstruction at the Catherine Palace is the famous Amber Room, with its amber wall panels created by German craftsmen, presented to Peter the Great in the early eighteenth century, stolen by the Nazis, and then lost. A small masterpiece by Rastrelli is the Cathedral of the Resurrection at the Smolny Convent, a Baroque confection in robin's egg blue and white. The one native Russian architect of the Baroque period whose work is comparable to Rastrelli's is Savva Chevakinsky, the designer of Petersburg's Cathedral of St. Nicholas.

The Neoclassical period that followed saw the end of ornate decoration and the introduction of clean, simple lines. The transition is easily seen in the area of the Smolny, where next to the Cathedral of the Resurrection stands the simple yellow Smolny Institute for Noblewomen, designed by Giacomo Quarenghi. The Smolny Institute, originally designed to provide education for girls, later served for a while as Lenin's headquarters. Charles Cameron designed a palace at Pavlovsk in the new, severe style.

In the early nineteenth century, the architect Carlo Rossi designed the gently curved General Staff Building and Arch which face the Winter Palace and Hermitage across a great open square. The arch is topped by a giant statue of a horse-drawn chariot. In the middle of the open square stands the Alexander Column, erected to commemorate the victory over Napoleon. The granite column topped with a figure holding a cross is more than 150 feet tall. Some of the major events in Russian history have taken place on this square, such as an infamous massacre of peaceful petitioners in 1905. Rossi also designed the Senate, near which is the most famous statue in all of Russia, the Bronze Horseman. The Bronze Horseman, designed by French sculptor Pierre-Étienne Falconet, shows Peter the Great seated on a horse which appears ready to leap off its stone base and race headlong across Russia. It was erected by Catherine II, the Great, in Peter's honor. Not far away rises the spire of the Admiralty, whose ornamentation instantly recalls Peter's desire for a navy in his new city. Designed by Andreyan Zakharov, it is one of the most distinctive buildings in St. Petersburg.

Both St. Petersburg and Moscow boast impressive houses erected during this period. Moscow, badly burned by the fire that raged during Napoleon's occupation of the city, needed extensive rebuilding after 1812. The huge Pashkov house, by Vasily Bazhenov, was among those needing repair. New houses designed by architects like Osip Bove were also erected. The victory over Napoleon was commemorated in Moscow by the enormous Church of Christ the Redeemer, designed by Konstantin Ton, who also planned the Grand Kremlin Palace, surely the most majestic "house" of the period. Both of these buildings show signs of a new movement to pay homage to Russia's past by incorporating design features from earlier periods. Some of the palace's rooms were decorated in an opulent Byzantine fashion, while the church, massive like St. Isaac's, sported domes and decorations in the old Russian style, rather than adhering to a Western style like St. Isaac's.

Other buildings continued this trend toward remembering the past. Vladimir Shervud's Historical Museum on Red Square at first glance looks like a typical Victorian-era pile, but it is adorned with towers, roofs, and decorations reminiscent of such churches as St. Basil's. In St. Petersburg, marking the spot where Alexander II was assassinated, the church of the Resurrection of the Savior on the Blood reminds the viewer of an opulent St. Basil's magically transported to this elegant city of classic, pastel buildings. Built during a time when an interest in Russian folk art was at its peak, it is the only building in central St. Petersburg that is at all reminiscent of the onion-domed churches so prevalent throughout the rest of Russia. At Abramtsevo, a group of artists of the new Arts and Crafts movement delved into the more distant past, creating the simple, charming church of the Icon of the Savior, drawing on the great architecture of the medieval period. The artist Viktor Vasnetsov drew on medieval manuscripts when designing the fanciful facade of the Tretyakov Gallery, the museum of Russian art in Moscow, in the early years of the twentieth century.

At the same time Vasnetsov was designing the Tretyakov Gallery facade, Fedor Shekhtel was consolidating his reputation as one of the leading archi-tects of the modern period. One of his best creations is the Ryabushinsky house, combining the new, square flat-roofed look associated with Frank Lloyd Wright with a heavy, curved entryway, adorned with art nouveau metalwork on the windows and front fence and mosaic work depicting flow-ers around the top. Inside a lush balustrade resembling successive waves, decorated with a medusa and lizards, leads up the curved stairway to the second floor. Shekhtel and other architects designed many new private homes and commercial buildings, and other structures such as railway stations, in Moscow and St. Petersburg in the decades before the 1917 revolution. Per-haps the most recognizable is the Singer Sewing Machine building on St. Petersburg's Nevsky Prospekt. Because there was a height restriction on buildings, the Singer building could not expect to loom high above other buildings on the street simply by adding floors. Instead, a tall slender dome capped by figures holding a globe with the Singer logo on it, all of which could be illuminated, caught the eye as it towered above the surrounding buildings, technically within the height restrictions because the dome was not habitable but only decorative. After the revolution, this building, like other private commercial enterprises, found other uses, in this case as the Dom Knigi, or House of Book, one of the finest bookstores in Russia.

Before the 1917 revolution, architects had worked in a number of styles, using elements from the Russian past as well as from the West, and occa-sionally adding ornamentation growing out of the Arts and Crafts movement. There had been a nod to Neoclassicism and also some interest in modern architecture. At the time of the revolution, there was for a while intense interest in creating something new and revolutionary in architecture just as in painting and the other arts. The best-known new movement was Constructivism, which attracted many of the best artists of the day. A famous early Constructivist design was for the Monument to the Third International by Vladimir Tatlin. It was to tower more than 1,300 feet, with three different levels in the form of a cube, a pyramid, and a cylinder, rotating once a year, once a day, and once a month. A model for the project was constructed, but ultimately the plan was rejected as unfeasible. A good example of Constructivist architecture that was actually built is the Zuev club, designed by Ilya Golosov in the late 1920s. Like Tatlin, Golosov based his design on geometric structures, in this case a harmonious combination of cubes and cylinders, clean curves and rectangles, with extensive use of glass and concrete, giving a distinctive modern, spare look to the building both inside and out. Other prominent architects of the period include the Vesnin brothers and Konstantin Melnikov, designer of the Rusakov Club. Another famous building of the period is Lenin's tomb on Red Square, its red granite cubes in stark contrast to the ornate St. Basil's to its right.

City planning became centralized and controlled in the 1930s. As in the other arts, it became dangerous to quarrel with official positions on architecture or to be seen as excessively concerned with formalism, that is, with the artistic form of a work rather than its content or function. Architects who wanted to work had to work under state supervision and conform to state guidelines, which left little room for experimentation or personal creativity.

The plans drawn up for city development were designed to improve the lives of the people, to beautify, and to glorify the regime. Ideally, people were to be housed in larger clusters that provided the necessities of life, and those groups would be part of larger and larger clusters that provided other services. Cities of the past traditionally had a center with services available there rather than spread evenly throughout the area, while the newer model was to eliminate the difference between the center and the edges of town by creating clusters with services for each group.

Creating new cities according to this plan was of course easier than modifying existing cities. In older cities like Moscow, buildings were torn down, unfortunately including many churches and decorated wooden houses; streets were widened; and parks were developed. The lavish Moscow subway was begun, and plans were laid for many new buildings.

World War II caused a setback in plans for the new Russia. The loss of life was enormous, as was the loss of buildings of all sorts. Postwar spending concentrated on rebuilding structures that were important to the Russian people like Peterhof, Peter I's estate outside Leningrad (St. Petersburg), and providing housing for the people, where the shortage was even more acute than it had been before the war. Some cities, including Stalingrad (now known as Volgograd), had been so devastated that they had to be rebuilt nearly from scratch.

During the postwar period, the buildings most identified with Stalin's regime were erected in Moscow. These were skyscrapers all built according to the same general plan, with a tall central rectangle topped by ever smaller structures and culminating in a spire. The rectangle was flanked by smaller wings. The style has been called Stalinist Gothic, or Stalinist wedding-cake. These buildings are dotted around Moscow, and are similar enough to surprise newcomers who are sure they have just seen the same building twenty minutes earlier across town. The buildings housed apartments, offices, hotels, a government ministry, and part of a university. The best known of the seven buildings are the Hotel Ukraina and the main building of Moscow State University on Sparrow Hills (Lenin Hills). The university building sits very high overlooking the city. The view from the overlook in front of the university is so magnificent that it attracts bridal parties for photographs.

The decades after Stalin's death in 1953 saw the construction of many apartments and other buildings, some of them shoddy, a result of speed, poor materials, and lack of training. The new Kalinin Prospekt cut through central Moscow, with its modern Scandinavian-looking buildings replacing many old houses and churches in a historic part of the city. A huge stadium arose near the university. The Ostankino television tower and the new hotel Rossiia, designed to house 6,000 guests at once, and sports facilities and hotels built in connection with the 1980 Olympics were other monuments of the period.

With the fall of communism in 1991, Moscow in particular began to take on a new look. Christ the Savior Cathedral, the Cathedral of Our Lady of Kazan, and Resurrection Gates, the latter two both on Red Square, were rebuilt. Inside the Kremlin, parts of the Palace of Facets and of the Grand Kremlin Palace, harmed by changes made during Stalinist times, were restored to their former beauty. Zurab Tsereteli was architect of much of the reconstruction of the city center and the creator of the controversial 184-foot statue of Peter the Great that was erected in Moscow. Plans were made for building facilities for shopping, business, banking, entertainment, and hosting tourists. Some of these projects never made it beyond the planning stages. Financing was always a problem, because Russia was short of funds and investment could be risky for foreigners. But a significant number of projects were realized. Old hotels were refurbished and were joined by new ones, often backed by Western money. GUM, Russia's premier department store on Red Square, changed from its drab Soviet incarnation into a showplace for all manner of Western goods from Kodak to Tampax, and in much the same way, Western money and Western institutions such as Marriott and McDonald's and Pizza Hut began to flood the city, joining the domestic projects underway. Statues to Dostoevsky, a writer neglected under communism, and to various other figures arose throughout the city. The subway system underwent repair and expansion, although the work was threatened by stoppages for financial reasons. The Bolshoi Theater appealed internationally for funding to repair and expand its facilities over a several-year period.

Other areas in Russia were faced with the same problems. The Hermitage in St. Petersburg received international assistance for its renovation, but smaller cities faced a bleaker outlook. Many small cities see their treasured buildings falling into disrepair through neglect or from the effects of pollution. They lack the means to repair the buildings and are searching for ways to attract money, with tourism a key source. Some like Yaroslavl are on the tourist route, seem well positioned to attract funding, and are taking steps to attract visitors. Yaroslavl is reconstructing a historic part of town and is re-creating an area like old-fashioned Russia with inns, craft workshops, and eating houses. Other more remote areas are not so fortunate, but are exploring ways to attract tourists with better hotel facilities and festivals.

Outside Moscow and St. Petersburg, Russia has several cities with the size and resources to succeed quite well in today's world. For instance, Nizhny Novgorod, a major city on the Volga River, has several building projects underway. Nizhny has a tradition of architectural excellence, and today its private workshops of architects are coming up with new creative designs for various types of buildings, especially housing. They are drawing on contemporary Western design but are also turning for inspiration to the Arts and Crafts and modernist movements of the pre-1917 period in Russia. In workshops like these may arise a new style of architecture that will characterize the new era dawning in postcommunist Russia.

SUGGESTED READINGS

Brumfield, William Craft. *A History of Russian Architecture*. Cambridge: Cambridge University Press, 1993.

Gerhart, Genevra. *The Russian's World: Life and Language*. New York: Holt, Rinehart, and Winston, 1994.

Hamilton, George Heard. *The Art and Architecture of Russia*. New Haven, CT: Yale University Press, 1983.

Russian Life magazine 7/96 for life at the dacha; 8–9/99 for Kizhi.

Glossary

Avoska.   Mesh shopping bag

Baba.   Woman, peasant woman; also a dessert

Babushka.   Grandmother

Balalaika.   Russian stringed instrument

Bliny.   Pancakes

Borscht.   Beet soup

Boyar.   Nobleman

Dacha.   House in the country used for vacations or weekends

Domovoi.   House spirit

Duma.   Parliament

Dvoryanin.   Nobleman

Fortochka.   Small window pane that can be opened for fresh air

Glasnost.   Openness

Icon.   Religious picture

Kasha.   Buckwheat groats

Kefir.   Milk product similar to yogurt

Kisel.   Fruit puree

Kokoshnik.   Woman's headdress

Kompot.   Compote, fruit dish

Kulebiaka.   Pie often stuffed with salmon

Kulich.   Easter cake

Kutia.   Ancient ritual food

Kvas.   Popular lightly fermented beverage

Leshii.   Forest spirit

Lukovitsa.   Onion dome

Maslenitsa.   Butter Week before Lent

Matryoshka.   Nesting doll

Mir.   Village collective

Oprichnina.   Administrative elite group established by Ivan the Terrible

Paskha.   Easter dessert

Pech.   Stove

Pelmeni.   Meat-filled dumplings

Perestroika.   Rebuilding

Pirozhki.   Meat pies

Ponyova.   Skirt

Rassolnik.   Soup with pickles

Riumka.   Small glass

Rossiisky.   Belonging to the Russian republic

Ruble.   Unit of Russian currency

Rusalka.   Water spirit

Russky.   Ethnically Russian

Samizdat.   Self-published work

Samovar.   Tea urn

Sarafan.   Jumper or pinafore

Shashlyk.   Shishkebab

Shchi.   Cabbage soup

Sirin.   Birdlike creature with a woman's face and breasts

Skazki.   Fairy tales

Sobornost.   Community of people united by love of the same values

Startsy.   Church elders

Steppe.   Plain, prairie

Taiga. Forest land

Troika. Conveyance pulled by three horses

Tsar (Czar). Ruler

Tundra. Land north of the tree line

Ukha. Fish soup

Vodianoi. Water spirit

Vodka. Alcoholic beverage

Yolka. Fir tree used for Christmas, New Year's

Yurodivy. Fool in Christ who gives up all possessions: believed to be able to prophesy

ZAGS. Marriage registry office

Zakuski. Appetizers

Zemsky sobor. Advisory group with representatives from various social groups

Bibliography

Afanas'ev, Aleksandr. *Russian Fairy Tales*. New York: Pantheon Books, 1973.

Barker, Adele Marie, ed. *Consuming Russia: Popular Culture, Sex, and Society since Gorbachev*. Durham, NC: Duke University Press, 1999.

Berdyaev, Nicolas. *The Russian Idea*. Boston: Beacon Press, 1962.

Berlin, Isaiah. *Russian Thinkers*. New York: Viking, 1978.

Billington, James H. *The Face of Russia*. New York: TV Books, 1998.

———. *The Icon and the Axe*. New York: Vintage, 1970.

Binyon, Michael. *Life in Russia*. New York: Berkeley Books, 1986.

Bird, Alan. *A History of Russian Painting*. Boston: G. K. Hall, 1987.

Boutenko, Irene A., and Kirill E. Razlogov, eds. *Recent Social Trends in Russia 1960–1995*. Montreal: McGill-Queen's University Press, 1997.

Boyd, Andrew. *An Atlas of World Affairs*. New York: Routledge, 1998.

Boym, Svetlana. *Common Places: Mythologies of Everyday Life in Russia*. Cambridge: Harvard University Press, 1994.

Brown, Archie, Michael Kaser, and Gerald S. Smith, eds. *The Cambridge Encyclopedia of Russia and the Former Soviet Union*. Cambridge: Cambridge University Press, 1994.

Brown, David, Gerald Abraham, and David Lloyd-Jones. *Russian Masters 1: Glinka, Borodin, Balakirev, Musorgsky, Tchaikovsky*. New York: W. W. Norton, 1986.

Brumfield, William Craft. *A History of Russian Architecture*. Cambridge: Cambridge University Press, 1993.

Chekhov, Anton. "Siren." In Avrahm Yarmolinsky, ed., *The Portable Chekhov*. New York: Viking, 1947.

Christmas in Russia. Lincolnwood, IL: Passport Books, 1993.

Clements, Barbara Evans, Barbara Alpern Engel, and Christine Worobec, eds. *Russia's Women*. Berkeley: University of California Press, 1991.

Creuziger, Clementine G. K. *Childhood in Russia: Representation and Reality*. New York: University Press of America, 1996.

Cushman, Thomas. *Notes from Underground: Rock Music Counterculture in Russia*. Albany: State University of New York Press, 1995.

Dabars, Zita. *The Russian Way*. Lincolnwood, IL: Passport, 1995.

De Tinguy, Anne, ed. *The Fall of the Soviet Empire*. Boulder, CO: East European Monographs, 1997.

Dutkina, Galina. *Moscow Days: Life and Hard Times in the New Russia*. New York: Kodansha International, 1996.

Edie, James M., James P. Scanlan, Mary-Barbara Zeldin. *Russian Philosophy*. Chicago: Quadrangle, 1965.

Epstein, Mikhail N., Alexander A. Genis, and Slobodanka M. Vladiv-Glover. *Russian Postmodernism*. New York: Berghahn Books, 1993.

Fedotov, G. P. *The Russian Religious Mind*. New York: Harper Torchbook, 1960.

Froncek, Thomas, ed. *The Horizon Book of the Arts of Russia*. New York: American Heritage, 1970.

Gaynor, Elizabeth, and Kari Haavisto. *Russian Houses*. New York: Stewart, Tabori, and Chang, 1991.

Gerhart, Genevra. *The Russian's World: Life and Language*. New York: Holt, Rinehart, and Winston, 1994.

Glad, Betty, and Eric Shiraev, eds. *The Russian Transformation: Political, Sociological, and Psychological Aspects*. New York: St. Martin's Press, 1999.

Glants, Musya, and Joyce Toomre, eds. *Food in Russian History and Culture*. Bloomington: Indiana University Press, 1997

Gogol, Nikolai. *Dead Souls*. Guilbert Guerney, trans. New York: Holt, Rinehart, and Winston, 1948.

Goldstein, Darra. *A La Russe: A Cookbook of Russian Hospitality*. New York: Random House, 1983. (Revised as *A Taste of Russia*, Montpelier, VT: Russian Information Services, 1999.)

Gorer, Geoffrey, and John Rickman. *The People of Great Russia: A Psychological Study*. New York: W. W. Norton, 1962.

Goscilo, Helena, and Beth Holmgren, eds. *Russia Women Culture*. Bloomington: Indiana University Press, 1996.

Gray, Camilla. *The Russian Experiment in Art 1863–1922*. London: Thames and Hudson, 1986.

Guerman, Mikhail. *Soviet Art 1920s–1930s*. New York: Harry N. Abrams, 1988.

Hamilton, George Heard. *The Art and Architecture of Russia*. New Haven, CT: Yale University Press, 1983.

Hansson, Carola, and Karin Liden. *Moscow Women*. New York: Pantheon, 1983.

Hare, Richard. *Pioneers of Russian Social Thought*. New York: Vintage, 1964.

Hecht, Leo. *The USSR Today: Facts and Interpretations*. Springfield, VA: Scholasticus, 1982.

Hilton, Alison. *Russian Folk Art*. Bloomington: Indiana University Press, 1995.

Hingley, Ronald. *The Russian Mind*. New York: Charles Scribner's Sons, 1977.

Hubbs, Joanna. *Mother Russia*. Bloomington: Indiana University Press, 1988.

Ivanits, Linda J. *Russian Folk Belief*. Armonk, NY: M. E. Sharpe, 1989.

Jack, Ian, ed. *Granta 64: Russia the Wild East*. New York: Viking Penguin, 1998.

Jones, Anthony, ed. *Education and Society in the New Russia*. Armonk, NY: M. E. Sharpe, 1994.

Kaiser, Robert G. *Russia: The People and the Power*. New York: Pocket Books, 1976.

Kalbouss, George. *Russian Culture*. Needham Heights, MA: Simon and Schuster, 1998.

Kelly, Catriona, and David Shepherd, eds. *Russian Cultural Studies*. New York: Oxford University Press, 1998.

Kirchner, Walther. *History of Russia*. New York: Barnes and Noble, 1963.

Kon, Igor, and James Riordan, eds. *Sex and Russian Society*. Bloomington: Indiana University Press, 1993.

Lahusen, Thomas, and Gene Kuperman. *Late Soviet Culture: From Perestroika to Novostroika*. Durham, NC: Duke University Press, 1993.

Lempert, David H. *Daily Life in a Crumbling Empire*. Boulder, CO: East European Monographs, 1996.

Leyda, Jay. *Kino: A History of the Russian and Soviet Film*. New York: Collier, 1973.

Lincoln, W. Bruce. *Between Heaven and Hell: The Story of a Thousand Years of Artistic Life in Russia*. New York: Viking, 1998.

Lossky, Nicholas O. *History of Russian Philosophy*. New York: International Universities Press, 1951.

Mackenzie, David, and Michael W. Curran. *A History of Russia and the Soviet Union*. Homewood, IL: Dorsey Press, 1977. (A 1998 update is titled *A History of Russia, the Soviet Union, and Beyond* and is published by Wadsworth Publishing Company.)

Mamonova, Tatyana. *Russian Women's Studies: Essays on Sexism in Russian Culture*. New York: Pergamon, 1989.

———, ed. *Women and Russia: Feminist Writings from the Soviet Union*. Boston: Beacon Press, 1984.

Marsh, Rosalind, ed. *Women in Russia and Ukraine*. Cambridge: Cambridge University Press, 1996.

Massie, Suzanne. *Land of the Firebird: The Beauty of Old Russia*. New York: Simon and Schuster, 1980.

McDowell, Bart. *Journey across Russia*. Washington, DC: National Geographic Society, 1977.

McPhee, John. *The Ransom of Russian Art*. New York: Farrar, Straus, Giroux, 1994.

Miller, Wright. *Russians as People*. New York: E. P. Dutton, 1961.

Milner-Gulland, Robin, and Nikolai Dejevsky. *Cultural Atlas of Russia and the Soviet Union*. New York: Facts on File, 1989.

Mirsky, D. S. *A History of Russian Literature*. New York: Alfred A. Knopf, 1966.

Moser, Charles, ed. *The Cambridge History of Russian Literature.* Cambridge: Cambridge University Press, 1996.

Moynahan, Bryan. *The Russian Century.* New York: Random House, 1994.

Murrell, Kathleen Berton. *Russia.* New York: Alfred A. Knopf, 1998.

Noble, John, Andrew Humphreys, Richard Nebesky, Nick Selby, George Wesely, and John King. *Lonely Planet Russia, Ukraine, and Belarus: Travel Survival Kit.* Oakland, CA: Lonely Planet, 1996.

Onassis, Jacqueline, ed. *In the Russian Style.* New York: Viking, 1976.

Papashvily, Helen, and George Papashvily. *Russian Cooking.* New York: Time-Life Books, 1969.

Pouncy, Carolyn Johnston, ed. *The Domostroi: Rules for Russian Households in the Time of Ivan the Terrible.* Ithaca, NY: Cornell University Press, 1994.

Reeder, Roberta, ed. *Russian Folk Lyrics.* Bloomington: Indiana University Press, 1993.

Remnick, David. *Resurrection: The Struggle for a New Russia.* New York: Random House, 1997.

Riasanovsky, Nicholas V. *A History of Russia.* New York: Oxford University Press, 1993.

Rice, Tamara Talbot. *A Concise History of Russian Art.* New York: Frederick A. Praeger, 1967.

Richmond, Yale. *From Nyet to Da: Understanding the Russians.* Yarmouth, ME: Intercultural Press, 1992.

Riha, Thomas. *Readings in Russian Civilization.* Chicago: University of Chicago Press, 1964.

Roosevelt, Priscilla. *Life on the Russian Country Estate.* New Haven, CT: Yale University Press, 1995.

Rosenthal, Bernice Glatzer. *The Occult in Russian and Soviet Culture.* Ithaca, NY: Cornell University Press, 1997.

Rozhnova, Polina. *A Russian Folk Calendar.* Moscow: Novosti, 1992.

Rzhevsky, Nicholas, ed. *The Cambridge Companion to Modern Russian Culture.* Cambridge: Cambridge University Press, 1998.

Service, Robert. *A History of Twentieth-Century Russia.* Cambridge: Harvard University Press, 1997.

Shaw, Denis J. B., ed. *The Post-Soviet Republics*: A Systematic Geography. Harlow, UK: Longman, 1996.

Shipler, David K. *Russia: Broken Idols, Solemn Dreams.* New York: Times Books, 1983.

Smith, Graham, ed. *The Nationalities Question in the Post-Soviet States.* New York: Longman, 1996.

Smith, Hedrick. *The Russians.* New York: Quadrangle, 1976.

Sokolov, Y. M. *Russian Folklore.* Detroit: Folklore Associates, 1971.

Soviet Almanac. New York: Harcourt Brace Jovanovich, 1981.

Stewart, John Massey. *The Nature of Russia.* New York: Cross River Press, 1992.

Stites, Richard. *Russian Popular Culture: Entertainment and Society since 1900*. Cambridge: Cambridge University Press, 1992.

———. *The Women's Liberation Movement in Russia*. Princeton, NJ: Princeton University Press, 1978.

Stone, Norman. *The Russian Chronicles: A Thousand Years That Changed the World*. New York: Quadrillion, 1998.

Sutherland, Jeanne. *Schooling in the New Russia*. New York: St. Martin's Press, 1999.

Terras, Victor. *A History of Russian Literature*. New Haven, CT: Yale University Press, 1991.

———. ed. *Handbook of Russian Literature*. New Haven, CT: Yale University Press, 1985.

Tian-Shanskaia, Olga Semyonova. *Village Life in Late Tsarist Russia*. Bloomington: Indiana University Press, 1993.

Tolstoy, Leo. *Anna Karenina*. New York: Penguin, 1978.

Toomre, Joyce. *Classic Russian Cooking: Elena Molokhovets' A Gift to Young Housewives*. Bloomington: Indiana University Press, 1983.

Troyat, Henri. *Daily Life in Russia under the Last Tsar*. Stanford, CA: Stanford University Press, 1961.

Tschizewskij, Dmitrij. *Russian Intellectual History*. Ann Arbor, MI: Ardis, 1978.

Vadrot, Claude-Marie. *Russia Today*. Wilmington, DE: Atomium Books, 1990.

Valkenier, Elizabeth. *Russian Realist Art*. Ann Arbor, MI: Ardis, 1977.

Visson, Lynn. *The Russian Heritage Cookbook*. Dana Point, CA: Casa Dana, 1998.

Volkov, Solomon. *St. Petersburg: A Cultural History*. New York: Free Press, 1995.

Volokh, Anne. *The Art of Russian Cuisine*. New York: Macmillan, 1983.

Von Bremzen, Anya, and John Welchman. *Please to the Table: The Russian Cookbook*. New York: Workman, 1990.

Vysokovskii, Aleksandr. *Stillborn Environments: The New Soviet Town of the 1960s and Urban Life in Russia Today*. Washington, DC: Kennan Institute, 1995.

Wagret, M. P. *U.S.S.R. Nagel's Encyclopedia-Guide*. Geneva: Nagel, 1973.

Wallace, Robert. *The Rise of Russia*. New York: Time-Life Books, 1967.

Ware, Timothy. *The Orthodox Church*. New York: Penguin Books, 1993.

Webber, Stephen L. *School, Reform, and Society in the New Russia*. New York: St. Martin's Press, 1999.

Wiens, Gerhard. *Beginning Russian Reader*. New York: Holt, Rinehart, and Winston, 1961.

Wilson, Drew, and Lloyd Donaldson. *Russian Etiquette and Ethics in Business*. Lincolnwood, IL: NTC Business Books, 1996.

Worobec, Christine D. *Peasant Russia: Family and Community in the Post-Emancipation Period*. DeKalb, IL: Northern Illinois University Press, 1995.

Zaletova, Lidya, Fabio Ciofi degli Atti, Franco Panzini, et al. *Revolutionary Costume*. New York: Rizzoli, 1989.

Zenkovsky, Serge A., ed. *Medieval Russia's Epics, Chronicles, and Tales*. New York: Dutton, 1974.

Zolotov, Andrei, Alexander Gusev, and Yelena Zonina. *The Bolshoi Theatre*. Moscow: Planeta, 1987.

Zorkaya, Neya. *The Illustrated History of the Soviet Cinema*. New York: Hippocrene Books, 1991.

OTHER RESOURCES

The Current Digest of the Post-Soviet Press

The Internet: good links can be found at *Russian Life*'s Top Ten Russia-related Websites (www.rispubs.com/rltop10.cfm); one excellent site is the Bucknell Russian Studies Department (www.departments.bucknell.edu/russian).

The New York Times has many good articles on Russia.

Russian Life magazine is a treasure of information about all things Russian.

Index

About the Author

SYDNEY SCHULTZE is Professor of Classical and Modern Languages at the University of Louisville, Louisville, Kentucky. She specializes in Russian literature, culture and language.